CATHERINE GROGNARD has been a dermatologist for twelve years. From an army family, she has always been keen on travelling and spent some time living with the Babinga pygmies in central Africa. During the course of her studies a nine month training period in the psychiatric service gave her an insight into the depths of the human soul. Her passion for tattoos arose from the chance discovery of a butterfly on the hip of a young woman referred to her because of an attack of urticaria. She has published Le Tatouage: Illustration, réparation (Arnette, 1991).

CLAUDIO LAZI, a promotional photographer from Germany, has lived in France since 1978. In December, 1990 he met up with his friend, Catherine Grognard, the dermatologist, and in April, 1991, at Elysée-Montmartre, he found himself surrounded by tattoos, tattooed and tattooists .....

This book grew out of a meeting between the authors and DOMINIQUE ISOIRD, who enjoyed designing it. The meeting was engineered by Lenny, a mutual friend with a passionate interest in ethnology. All they needed was an opportunity, which eventually materialised in the form of an invitation to the first international tattooing convention, organised by the AFT (Association française du tatouage/French Tattooing Association) at the Elysée-Montmartre in Paris.

ISBN 0-681-00577-7

Printed and Bound in Spain

First Longmeadow Press Edition
0 9 8 7 6 5 4 3 2 1

THE TATTOO

LONGMEADOW
PRESS

GRAFFITI FOR THE SOUL

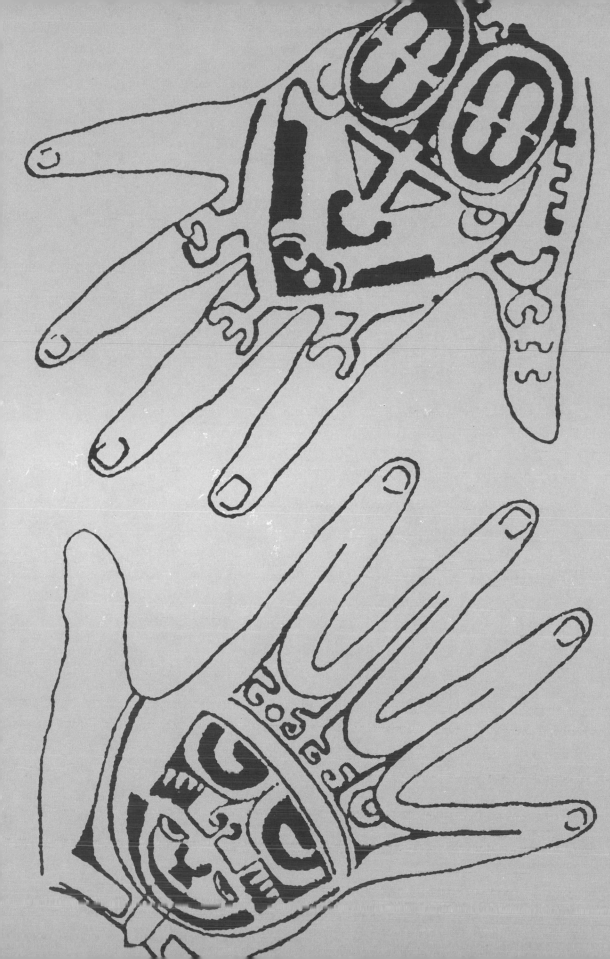

Stratagem, strategy, the madness of lust - tattooing is more than just a design on the skin - it is a function, a process. Dr. Grognard will never conclude her investigation of the skin. Here she provides both written and visual material and conducts a tenacious quest for knowledge of the skin - a tissue whose embryology is synonymous with memory. The doctor often diverts from the main theme to address topics of intellectual curiosity and to question the human condition. For what is one to make of this violation of tissue at the hand of the artist, the exploitation of the skin as a haven for drifting continents? The tattooed person is reclothed in and anointed by the pictorial ointment.

Gradually, forcefully, the graphics are realised, revealing the art of a master and a job well done. The scope of this work covers every aspect of the subject, from the origins of the skin and the writings expressed on it, right through to the restoration of the empty page by the mysterious laser.

Doctor Catherine Grognard guides us through the entire spectrum of this language which uses the flesh as a background. The suppleness of the skin, the richness of the transitory object which it represents. What should be done with this prize which we hold? Decorate it again and again with different motifs which are apparently rooted in our consciousness, but in fact arise from the depths of our subconcious - mysterious alchemy ......

As soon as you start reading this book, you will become submerged in its pages. The next time you pick it up, read between the lines, for that is where you will find the true thoughts of the author.

ETIENNE FROGÉ
Professor of Legal Medicine - Vice President of the French Legal Medicine and Criminology Society

Throughout the ages, in almost every corner of the world, tattooing is accompanied by the smell of brimstone and has expressed suffering, evil and death. So it is not insignificant that it is a young and vibrant woman, Catherine Grognard, who now sheds some light on this shadowy world of skin transfer madness, on the art of tattooing.

In some ways this form of expression holds litle hope, in so far as one loses a part of one's true self by modifying the original covering of skin.

For didn't the French convicts of the last century refer to tattoos as "bouzilles" - botch jobs? The colour green was predominant because it symbolised escape, the positive; and also because it was the only colour which the prison authorities did not supply to the metropolitan prisons, where red and yellow were the main colours in the regulation uniforms. "The past betrayed me, the present torments me, the future fills me with dread" were the sentiments tattooed on the body of a convict from Cayenne. But, as Catherine Grognard demonstrates, tattooing also plays a strong and much more positive role in initiation rites.

Having spent a long time living in the Pacific region, I saw many of these creations of the skin and I realised that they flourished during times of crisis, especially in New Caledonia, where recent events have sparked off a renaissance of traditional tattooing (carried out in the past by using bamboo "wool" and abrasive herbs). Young Melanesians have independence slogans tattooed on their backs, and even the portrait of Eloi Machoro - one of their fallen leaders. Tattoo art is also secret art, in that it does not have to be visible, and is only exposed if the bearer of the tattoo wishes to reveal it. It is a phenomenon which is similar to moulting or shedding of skin and therefore it is hardly surprising that the serpent, the incarnation of evil in the Garden of Eden and also a sexual symbol, is frequently to be seen in torrid visual representations. Indeed the reptile itself, its skin stamped with quasi-geometrical motifs, could be described as the first creature tattooed by nature.

The potentially bleak study of this subject is made more light-hearted by the author's collection of photographs. A book of images which are stuck to the skin, dragons of the flesh, lascivious serpents hissing on the breasts, these rich examples of the martyred skin incite the reader to marvel at their brutal beauty, their tormented graphics and their vibrant primary colours.

This is a courage one wishes were displayed by the young people who deface the walls and the tube stations with their signs. They would be so much more revolutionary if they wore their graffiti on their own flesh.

A.D.G.
Journalist

GRAFFITI FOR THE SOUL

BY CATHERINE GROGNARD

PHOTOGRAPHY BY

CLAUDIO LAZI

THE SKIN

"Do not mock the deeds and actions of others, do not deplore them or judge them, but try to understand them." SPINOZA

The very soul can be read on the open page of the skin......

A worn or torn envelope, a reflection of desires fulfilled or frustrated emotions, it is weathered by time to become a priceless parchment, rewritten thousands of times to mirror the experiences of the bearer.

Its function is not only that of a bark or a crust, a simple physical barrier against hostile, external forces. It is not a mere game-bag of organs and muscles, but a valuable transitional organ in its own right.

Both screen and means of communication, the role of the skin is that of protector, intermediary or go-between. In delineating the boundaries of the self, it acts as a means of exchange with others.

The skin reveals to man the sensual universe and makes him aware that he exists. The skin offers itself to the eye, which caresses it from afar, probes covertly and unveils. To talk of having nerves skin deep (the French term for being on edge) is therefore not just an abstract expression, but a tangible reality.

The skin is a multi-coloured, socio-cultural language. Above all it talks to the doctor, and dermatology presents us with a vast range of psychological conflicts and signs of man's torment projected onto the outer envelope. The skin - rosy, smooth and supple, like that of a child - can radiate health and happiness, but can also indicate sickness and misery when it is painful, rough and bruised. Pale and cold, it has a deathly appearance. Everything points to something - one just has to know how to look.

Stress and anxiety take the form of white scabs or red weals on the skin. Impatience, itches and goose bumps are an expression of repulsion. These itching diseases, aggravated and sustained by the urge to scratch, transform pain into a pleasure which is almost erotic, and culminates in climactic relief, trapping the person who is compelled to scratch in a cycle of dependence.

There is also a psychoanalytical interpretation. The

communicator of well-being, seduction and emotion, the skin is the mirror of the soul, exposing pleasure as well as pain. According to Anzieu "it reveals itself as a fragile envelope which is open to both physical and psychic penetration." Anzieu also wonders whether the "pyschic paradox is not supported to a certain extent by the nature of the skin..." This skin, both permeable and impenetrable, ally and traitor, protects human nature in its folds, but, on the other hand, it could just as easily expose the most intimate secrets of this fragile entity.

Is there a link between the skin and the brain? The answer lies in embryology, for they both originate from the same tissue.

From the very first month of gestation, in the womb, the embryo is covered with ectoderm. This membrane envelops the skin, the sensory organs and the brain. Then, at a later stage, the brain merges with the nerves to form the grey matter of the foetus; the skin is excluded from this process, but maintains its close connections with the brain. At the moment of birth, when the baby is suddenly expelled from the soft, warm cocoon, its first contact with the outside world is epidermal. The newborn is surrounded by a strange, cold and hostile world and shivers. Like a drowning man resurfacing, he takes a breath, utters a cry and then calms down as he re-establishes contact with his mother's skin, whose vibrations are so familiar to him. Thus pain and pleasure are contained in a series of tactile sensations, like invisible tattoos. From the moment of birth these tattoos delineate the limits of the body, by transmitting to the brain messages which are both tangible and imperceptible. The body learns how to feel through contact with external objects. It learns of others.

In the course of life we become aware of a barrier between the internal (the self) and the external (others). We can manipulate this barrier as we wish, by opting for fusion or distance.

We try to set our own individual limits, and, in seeking to be different, we mark ourselves to stand out from our environment.

For thousands of years tattooing has helped us to fulfil these aspirations, conveying its unique socio-cultural message. The Caduveo Indians felt foolish without decorations, the Mayas tattooed themselves to become closer to supernatural beings and would disfigure themselves to the point of ugliness to distance themselves from humanity and to become more mysterious and frightening, like gods. Without their scarifications the Bafia of Cameroon feel that they are on a level with chimpanzees or pigs. In south east Zaire, the women of the Tabwa tribe are not allowed to marry before they have undergone the ritual scarification. From tribal incisions to more sophisticated etched paintings, this type of calligraphy is universal. In 20th century western society, tattooing is more than a simple decoration, admired by some and criticised or rejected by others - it is a cry of the soul which tears the skin.

The naked body is a body without conversation. The language of the skin presents a means of expression which is simple and accessible to everyone, where the image replaces the word. Its range of artifices enables us to modify our personality. As if, feeling claustrophobic in our little shell, we seek to extend it by means of visual subterfuge. This desire to transcend the limits finds form in a mixture of pleasure and pain. As the saying goes: "One must suffer in order to be beautiful"...... and, it is tempting to add, desirable. Clothes and accessories can be removed and replaced, make-up is transitory, but tattooing necessitates total commitment. It is a life-long engagement; the skin can't be changed like a shirt.

The stereotype of the tattooed person is typically someone who belongs to a marginal group, such as hippy, punk or biker, all of whom flaunt their rejection of the system. The teenage rebel models himself on the criminal and the characters of the underworld to look hard and gain street credibility.

All these factors sustain the long-standing negative image of tattooing. But the perception of tattooing is not limited to this narrow-minded view. Rich in symbolic value, the image undeniably unleashes a magical power. The large, panoramic tattoos are often true works of art. These naive images bathe the body in colours, presenting a fascinating sight.

The astonished beholder is lost in an unfamiliar world, and, possibly, outraged at first, but he is gradually seduced by it. But isn't it the case that the world of tattooing revolves around this perverse game in which the beholder is intent on fulfilling his desire to see what the bearer does not really want to reveal? The person who is tattooed lets the beholder make his own interpretation without really compromising himself. The protagonists become secret accomplices. Were it not for this tacit connivance, this potentially erotic communication could be transformed into an obscene provocation, making the observer feel uncomfortable. It is only the onlooker's gaze which enables delivery of the message, maintains the illusion and justifies the artifice. "The regard of others is enough for me to be who I am, not for myself, certainly, but for others," wrote Jean-Paul Sartre.

The symbolic value of tattooing is interpreted in different ways by different people according to their tastes, ideas, anxieties.......

There is nevertheless a common thread: the necessity of existing, of feeling oneself to be unique and maybe immortal....

Indeed, the tattoo, the sign, remains until putrefaction, and even longer, if the skin is preserved (tanned).

So, to a certain extent, the tattoo can alleviate existential anguish. The tattooed person belongs to the group of protestors who denounce the ultimate scandal: death!

THE HISTORY OF TATTOOING

Tattooing, man's first form of writing, is the most ancient and universal mode of symbolic expression. It appears to be linked to man's evolution and to the development of awareness of "the self." It illustrates, according to Levi-Strauss, "the transition from a natural to a cultural state." These lines, dots and more elaborate drawings are an indication of man's desire to tell his story.

All the nomadic peoples try to distinguish themselves from the rest, to make themselves unique and also to establish a means of recognising their kinsmen in the various clans. In order to achieve this, they resort to the resource which is the most accessible and the most lasting: their skin. This decorated skin defines the boundary against the hostility of the outside world,for it is visible to everyone and it accompanies the individual everywhere.

Of course, it is impossible to prove that body adornment dates back to prehistoric times, but there are indications that this is the case. Neanderthal man used red ochre to inscribe a pattern on the bones of the dead. This procedure was linked to the idea of survival: red ochre, the colour of blood, symbolised life.

Prehistoric remains, such as the cave paintings of Lascaux and Eyzies in the Dordogne, are proof of this early inclination towards adornment and decoration. The body of the Vénus Impudique (the Shameless Venus), dating from the middle Magdalenian period, and kept in the Musée de l'Homme, is covered with red ochre marks. There are more conspicuous examples of tattooing techniques on the parietal paintings of the Sahara, and on Egyptian statues dating from the 5th millenium. The oldest mummified tattoo is without doubt that of the priestess of Hathor, from the 11th dynasty of ancient Egypt, which dates back to 2,200 BC. The famous horned goddess of Tassili N'Ajjer (Inaouanrhat) bears evidence of body adornment which appears to be a type of scarification on her

The tattoo is intriguing, and can sometimes be disconcerting, but it rarely provokes an indifferent reaction. This universal language, embedded in the skin, dates back to the very beginning of man's history. It is a language of colours which transforms the body into an image to convey a message to those who know how to look..........

shoulders, breasts, thighs and calves. The figurine of Nagada and Ballas from the upper Nile [1] bears black zig-zag motifs on a red ochre background - a sign of fertility. Numerous Egyptian, [2] Peruvian and Asian mummies also have marks on their bodies.

It seems probable, therefore, that man has tattooed himself throughout the ages, motivated by the need for a symbolic affirmation of his human status, as well as by a desire to adorn himself.

Throughout its history, tattooing has been endowed with religious, military and initiation -or rites of passage - symbolism.

The Gauls of Brittany and the Picts derived their names from the art of tattooing. The name "Pict" is the Latin translation (picti) of the indigenous Celtic word "brith" (or "breiz"), which means paint. [3] The Roman soldiers gave the name Picts to the Gallic soldiers who had a tradition of undressing in preparation for battle. They did this to relieve themselves of their burdensome clothes, but, in so doing, they exposed to their astonished enemies their tattooed bodies, covered with tribal symbols and mascots.

In the Middle East and Europe tattooing became less common with the establishment of the large Barbaric empires. It was only practised after that by the Scythian nomads of the eastern steppe land. This was proved in 1947 by the discovery of the body of a Scythian man, covered in tattoos. This body had been mummified by the ice, probably in the 5th century BC, in a prehistoric burial chamber at Pazyrik in the Altai Mountains. [4]

It is believed that these lavish decorations were designed to complement the clothing worn at that time, and that they also fulfilled the role of a magical protector.

The origins of the anxiety generated by tattoos today, particularly in western cultures, are rooted in the Bible and the Christian religion. The body, created in God's image, is the temple of the soul. Therefore it should not be violated. Unfortunately religious texts are not always unambiguous with regard to this subject.

The Book of Revelation of St. John refers to a sign which Jehovah allowed the Hebrews to etch on their faces. This was the tau cross, which is the divine seal in the Judeo-Christian religion, the sign of the chosen people. It is represented by a "T" which the Hebrews wore on their foreheads when they fled to the promised land.

Other texts state that tattooing was forbidden as soon as the Hebrews - who were formerly Egyptian slaves and therefore marked to indicate this - departed from Egypt with Moses.

Verse xxviii, chapter XIX of Leviticus says: "You shall not make any cuttings in your flesh on account of the dead or tattoo any marks upon you: I am the Lord."

The first Christians in Gaul started tattooing again, particularly the form of a cross, as a sign of recognition to each other, but it was condemned by the church in the Middle Ages as an idolatrous, superstitious and barbaric practice. The Middle Ages was an era pervaded by great fear and intense mysticism, and tattoos were considered to be the works of the devil.

For the Copts, Buddhists and Indians, the everlasting nature of tattooing also enabled them to reach beyond this world, but in a positive way. For them it was an element of the religious ritual. However, on the contrary, in the Koran, tattoos are considered to be evil. They make it impossible for the tattooed person to pray properly, since one should purify oneself by washing prior to prayer, and these ablutions, of course, cannot cleanse the skin of tattoos.

Throughout the ages these marks on the body have retained an ambivalent character. The inscription indicates a system of classification and reveals the difference between the believers and the others, the pure and the impure, the free man and the slave or prisoner, the woman and the prostitute, the upright man and the rogue. Whether it is an emblem of worth or of infamy, the tattoo symbolis-

1 Kept at the Ashmolean Museum in Oxford, UK.

2 In 1923 H.E. Winlock discovered two mummies from the 2nd dynasty in a tomb at Deir El-Bahary. They were tattooed on the arms, legs, soles of the feet and pubic area.

3 According to Le Nouveau Larousse Illustré. However it should be noted that the etymology of these words has not been corroborated by linguists.

4 Mountainous region in southern Siberia, close to the Mongolian border.

es that one belongs to a certain group or profession.

Slaves have been tattooed since antiquity. This identifying sign on the forehead could be hidden by the hair, so it was later placed between the eyes. The Romans mockingly called the slaves "men of letters." A proverb from this era even stated that there was no-one more well-read than a Samian, because, apparently, the slaves brought from Samos, or possibly from Samothrace, were extensively tattooed. They were also called the caelatos - the engraved - because their bodies resembled inlaid works of art. In the African slave trade the identificaton mark was branded on the breast with a red hot iron. According to article 38 of the "Black Code" written by Colbert, and published shortly after his death in 1685, "Runaway black slaves are marked with a fleur-de-lis to show that they belong to a master and are the property of the state itself." This type of mark was also used by the French penal system until the First Empire. Thieves were identified by a fleur-de-lis [5] or the letter "V" tattooed on the right shoulder, and galley slaves by the three letters "GAL." Although the decision to terminate this practice was taken in 1832, it was not until twenty years later that it was finally replaced by printed police records. The Greeks also undertook a similar practice by branding their prisoners with an owl - the bird dedicated to the goddess Minerva.

At the time of the French Revolution there was a craze for tattooing in certain circles, although those who were tattooed risked being embarrassed by this spontaneous gesture in later years. There is a well-known story of Bernadotte, who had "Death to the King" tattooed on his left arm when he was a young republican lieutenant and passionate Jacobin revolutionary. Years later, having been crowned King of Sweden in 1810, he had to uncover his arm to undergo blood-letting for an attack of uraemia. The doctor was stunned by the provocative inscription. There is no record of the reaction of Desirée Clary, who married Bernadotte after Emperor

Napoleon I had left her, nor of his loyal valet, who was sworn to secrecy.

Prisoners in the Nazi concentration camps were also branded like animals. A registration number, corresponding to the camp, was stamped [6] on the left forearm. This was preceded by a "D" if the person was Jewish.

Tattoos signifying affiliation to certain groups also existed alongside those which indicated slavery, imprisonment or infamy.

Roman soldiers would inscribe the name of their general or a drawing of a sparrow-hawk (a symbol of their military function) on the back of their hand. Similarly, twenty centuries later, Goebbels suggested to Hitler that members of the SS should have the letters "SS" followed by their blood type tattooed under the left armpit, to ensure that they received preferential medical treatment if they were wounded. However, this procedure also made it possible to identify deserters and, in the post-war years, former Nazis, for, given the location of the tattoo, a scar was just as revealing as the original mark..... In France, the old legionnaires of the African and Indochina battalions are proud of their skin decorations.

The chronicles of Herodotus revealed that, in ancient Greece, some leading citizens and those in positions of power were tattooed; for example, architects with a triangle on the left bicep, priests with a sun on the thigh and interpreters with a parrot on the chest. In Nubia and ancient Egypt musicians, dancers and prostitutes were tattooed with an erotic pattern on the pubis and thighs.

These customs were probably the forerunners of the professional labels which were to develop, in particular amongst the French craftsmen, who bore the insignia of their profession on their biceps like the firemen, coolies and litter-bearers of Japan. These craftsmen, or journeymen, would travel from town to town to ply their trade. In the absence of a diploma, which could, in any case, be lost or forged, they bore proof of their qualification on their skin.

5 *Milady de Winter was tattooed with a fleur-de-lis in Alexandre Dumas' novel The Three Musketeers.*

6 *The stamp contained removable numbers and letters made up of tiny needles, which were dipped in ink before being injected into the skin.*

Furthermore, this method of identification enabled them to find work throughout Europe, regardless of their ability to speak the language of the country they were in. In the Dechambre dictionary Professor Lacassagne provides a list of the insignia of these craftsmen. For example:

- Stone carvers, the initiators of the tradition, wear compasses, a right-angle, a chisel and a plumb line
- Carpenters display a plane and pliers
- Butchers: a bull's head on crossed knives
- Bakers: scales, kneading trough and a loaf
- Barbers: comb and crossed scissors
- Cobblers: an awl and a boot
- Blacksmiths: an anvil and a hammer
- Sailors: an anchor
- Vine-growers: a bunch of grapes
- Gunsmiths: a pistol

In 1791, a revolutionary law (the Le Chapelier law) resulting from the Allard Decree abolished these guilds of craftsmen. Gradually the journeyman's emblems were forgotten. Only a few passionate craftsmen refused to let them go. And it is still possible to find craftsmen who remain loyal to this tradition and bear a tattoo which indicates their journeyman status.

It was the accounts of the great sea voyages around this time which sparked off a resurgence of interest in tattooing. Captains and sailors related tales of their voyages to the distant shores of the Pacific islands, and displayed the souvenirs of these expeditions engraved on their skin. It was Captain James Cook who first discovered the tattooed people of this region. [7] He described the natives of Tahiti in his diary in July, 1769: "The men and women paint their bodies. In their language, this is called tatau. They do it by injecting an indelible black pigment under the skin." The tatau of the Tahiti princes, the tiki [8] of the Marquesans, the moko of the Maori chiefs and the pa of the Papuans became objects of envy. In the 16th century, the Europeans who had discovered the New World were also

influenced by and began to participate in the tattooing practices of the American Indians. But not everyone condoned this trend. The missionaries were suspicious of these barbaric signs which defaced the work of God. P. Dubé recorded the advice given by a concerned Christian man to his son, who was about to embark for America: "Do not submit to licentiousness and beware of the madness of pricking yourself. I forbid it. Remember that these are the words of your loving father and heed what he has written here." [9] Colonial expansion, the increase in travel, the invention of photography and the growth of the media all played a role in the increase in popularity of tattooing at this time.

Even the bourgeoisie and the nobility were infatuated with this form of self-adornment. It was the young Prince of Wales, the future King Edward VII, who endorsed tattooing for the nobility. The English gentry rushed to emulate Queen Victoria's children, who were tattooed during a trip to Yokohama in Japan in 1882. The London tattooists, including Tom Riley, George Burchett, known as "the king of tattooists, the tattooist of kings," and especially Sutherland MacDonald, the "Raphael" of tattooists, were widely acknowledged as the best in the field. Sutherland MacDonald was particularly skilled in the Japanese art of tattooing, and used more than twenty colours and shades to create a brilliant, vivid effect which was much admired. His clients included Edward VII, George II of Greece, Tsar Nicholas, the King of Denmark and the Sultan of Jahore.

Many of the great Chinese and Japanese masters of the art of tattooing moved to the west to satisfy the growing demand there. They opened salons in the large ports and the major cities - New York, San Francisco, London, Hamburg - and soon gained a worldwide reputation amongst tattooing enthusiasts.

Having been restricted to the lower classes of society and to the geishas for a long time, Japanese tattooing was awarded fine art status in the 13th

7 During the Endeavour's maiden voyage (1768-1771), Cook explored the Pacific Ocean and discovered the Marquesas Islands, the Society Islands, New Zealand and New Holland, or Australia. He returned to England via the Indian Ocean to prove to his contemporaries that a southern continent did indeed exist.

8 In Polynesian Tiki means "chief" and also "son of the sun." It is Tiki who supposedly taught man the art of tattooing and the totem was also named after him.

9 P. Dubé: Tattoo, tatoué - Montreal, Jean Basile, 1980, page 34.

century, during the Edo period. However it remained predominantly a lower class practice, utilised by marginal groups as a form of protest against the strict rules of the feared Togugawa Kakufu military regime. However various professional groups were also very fond of this type of adornment. The Kabuki actors [10] used tattoos to get into the parts which they were playing and to enhance the role. The litter-bearers used tattoos as a way of attracting custom. Their colourful bodies served as their uniform. The Japanese fishermen believed that they could protect themselves from dangerous fish by wearing a tattoo on their leg. As for the Japanese firemen, they played a significant role both in the history of tattooing and in the history of Japan itself. The frequent outbreaks of fire in the towns constructed from wood and paper required an efficient and courageous fire-fighting force. The members of these forces were easily identified by their special, richly coloured coats, decorated with gaudy dragons and spiralling clouds. These decorations and motifs were repeated in tattoos under the coats, and these tattoos were regarded both as a form of medal for bravery in the face of fire, and as a symbolic protection against the dangers faced by the firemen. As well as being a symbol of power and god of thunder, the dragon was a hybrid creature, embracing elements of both fire and water. Those fire-fighters who bore the dragon's image enjoyed a privileged status. The soldiers also tattooed themselves to appear tough and war-like, and to emulate the hero of *Suikoden*. This novel, taken from a Chinese literary work in 90 volumes, illustrated by the master engraver, Hokusi, relates the tale of a tattooed rebel chief, who took on the role of protector of the oppressed. His chivalrous deeds and preachings on the virtue of honour were much admired and boosted the development of body art. Tattooing, along with engraving, subsequently became one of the most popular and representative art forms of Japan. However this worried the Japanese authorities, who feared that

body art would discredit the country in the eyes of the western countries with which they had established new and lucrative economic and trade relations. As a result, tattooing was forbidden by Emperor Meiji during the 1870s. However the Europeans, impressed by the rich imagery and colours, did not reject body art in the slightest. On the contrary, they soon joined the clientele of the master tattooists, thereby ensuring the spread of popularity of tattooing worldwide. In 1945, after the defeat of Japan and the arrival of the US forces, tattooing was legalised again, although it was still not necessarily considered socially acceptable at that time. Today, in Japan, it is only practised by a small group of the population, most of whom belong to some sort of closed club. The most famous of these is the Yakusa, a crime syndicate similar to the Mafia.

The Yakusa deliberately designed their tattoo, which usually covered the whole body, to stop at the wrist and at the knee. Until the middle of the 20th century, the authorities did not condone the practice of tattooing, and punishment was severe, so the tattooists made sure that they avoided any exposed parts of the body. Those who took the risk of being tattooed entered into a written agreement with the tattooist on the theme, based on the amount of money they had to spend. There is still a binding contract between the artist and the client, although it is not written or verbalised. Tattooing follows a precise ritual and the colours used - red, green indigo and yellow - are the four colours of the art of engraving. The different shades of these colours are achieved by mixing or diluting the inks. Tattooing is still carried out manually, mixing pain and pleasure. Both slowness and silence are part of the ritual. Tea breaks and hot baths are the only interruptions during the sessions. The creation of these luxurious "skin costumes" can take years. This ritualistic eastern approach differs from the less methodical and more timid European attitude towards tattooing. Unlike the eastern fresco approach, undertaken by one tattooist, the western

10 The Kabuki Theatre was founded during the 12th century in Kyoto and later moved to Edo. The actors expressed themselves by means of their body art, whereby the graphics were chosen from a repertoire of motifs and the colours adhered to the rigid code of yin/yang symbolism.

tattoo is a collage of small images, usually assembled randomly to record emotional or physical journeys, and carried out by a number of different tattooists.

Up until the end of the 19th century many tattooed Europeans would display their bodies at circuses and fairs, alongside nature's "monsters," such as bearded ladies and Siamese twins. In the USA the Barnum Circus was famous for its Living Picture Gallery, which featured Prince Constantin, a Greek who boasted 388 different tattoos. In France, Edmond Faucher claimed to be the most tattooed man in the world - "the living goblin" - and charged the curious 50 centimes for a viewing. In addition to the tattoos on the palms of his hands, the insides of his ears and his tongue, he bore an immense fresco depicting a fox-hunting scene, which started on his chest and ended, with the kill, on his thigh. The so-called "Ricardo," formerly with the African Battalion, exhibited himself at the Santander Fair in Spain, after serving a twenty year sentence of hard labour for murder, and recounted how it had taken six years for him to be completely tattooed. Women then began to steal the limelight - for example, Salome, the "blue lady" who was apparently an oriental beauty tattooed in fourteen colours. These men and women who exhibited their tattoos added to the exotic attraction by making up incredible stories, in which, captured by savages, they are tattooed against their will, endure immense suffering and are saved only by their strength and courage...

The British, pioneers of the art of tattooing until the beginning of the 20th century, found themselves in competition with the Americans soon after that. One of the reasons for this sudden trans-Atlantic development in the art was undoubtedly Samuel O'Reilly's invention of the electric tattooing machine. This machine revolutionised tattooing technique. In the large cities and the ports, ship's anchors and pin-up girls stretched out lasciviously on bulging biceps once more conjured up the image of a world outside decent society. Macho vulgarity triumphed over refinement and good taste, and tat-

tooing was once again the preserve of dubious, marginal groups, reinstating the challenge to social conventions.

Periodically tattooing comes back into fashion. However, whatever its fashionable status, it has always been widespread amongst marginal groups. In England, in the 1950s, the teddy boys and rockers gave it a new lease of life. Then, in the 1960s, the hippies started to take an interest in distant cultures, viewing them in a different way from the earlier colonials, who were only interested in the practices and beliefs of the countries which they settled in order to govern them more effectively. The hippies, on the other hand, would immerse themselves in the way of life of the selected country, usually Asian, [11] in order to identify with it and actually become a part of it, having rejected the values of their own culture. For them these Asian people, their distant brothers, had succeeded where their own society had failed, in retaining the true, simple values of humanity. Tattooing, as well as ear and nose piercing, in Hindu style, was a part of this integration process. The Hell's Angels adopted tattooing as a rallying sign similar to the badges worn on their leather jackets. Winged, helmeted skulls and huge eagles are part of the Hell's Angels' uniform, alongside other accessories, such as silver and turquoise Navajo rings and, of course, the impressive, indispensible Harley-Davidson. In the 1980s punks changed their appearance in the most outrageous way possible to flaunt all the conventions. Loud colours, anarchic haircuts, pierced noses, ears and lips; head, arms and legs tattooed with skulls, swastikas and neo-Nazi slogans - all these were deliberately provocative to demonstrate their attitude of hatred, their arrogance and their desire to shock through violence.

All these forms of body art - practised by teddy boys, rockers, hippies, Hell's Angels and punks - arose as a protest against some sort of cultural uniformity. The ease with which one can travel abroad nowadays, the mixing of different races, and, above

11 For the hippies from the USA, this might also have been an attempt at reintegration in this region following the Vietnam War.

12 Made between the two World Wars.

13 Filmed in 1968.

all, the power of the media have created an anonymous, international style, which threatens to lead to the loss of our local, national or traditional identity. It is ironic to see that avant-garde artists are increasingly reverting to the wealth of designs offered by primitive tattoos and other forms of body decoration - forms which, for centuries, our society has tried to conceal beneath so-called civilisation.

In France, films like *Pépé le Moko* [12] with Jean Gabin - who featured again thirty years later in Denis de La Patelière's *Le Tatoué* [13] - or, more recently, Yochi Takabayashi's *The Tattooed Woman* [14] led to a resurgence of tattooing. Celebrities and even politicians were tattooed, Lenin, Stalin, Roosevelt, Churchill, Marshall Montgomery and Tito being some of the most famous. [15] It was said that Count Tolstoy took great pleasure in unveiling his tattoos at the end of dinner parties. More recently, the showbusiness world has taken up tattooing in a big way. It's all a question of fashion - what's "in". Gérard Depardieu, Cher, Béatrice Dalle, Sean Connery and many others belong to the "brotherhood." Congresses and competitions are organised, where tattooists come to discuss and improve their techniques and the tattooed exhibit their designs and look for ideas for new motifs. These events attract curious observers, some of whom succumb to temptation and depart adorned with a butterfly, flower or jaguar - the beginnings of a future fresco.

Nevertheless, since the end of the last century, tattooing has usually been viewed with disapproval. Regardless of the fact that certain celebrities bear a tattoo as a mark of originality and individuality, for most people it remains a suspicious sign, linked to marginal, not entirely above board groups. Tattooing is considered by the majority to be somehow immoral. The well-known Italian criminologist, Cesare Lombroso, included in his work on the criminal man a profile of the delinquent. In this he presents tattooing as an indication of a rebellious adolescence, and, furthermore, as a sign of an asocial and menacing attitude. Alexander Lacassagne, an army surgeon and subsequently a professor in Lyon, came to the same conclusion. Juvenile delinquents and prisoners had a reputation for "pricking their hide." They communicate by means of that which is most precious to them: their skin, for which they will fight to the death. Cynically they display slogans such as "No luck," "Born to suffer," "No god, no master" and "Beaten but not tamed" to cope with the anguish of guilt or inferiority complexes. Tattooing is called "the convict's flower" in French slang, and this reflects the view that it is above all a language of defiance.

Similar to graffiti, tattooing is a means of expression for the individual who is seeking a way to break free from the repression of society. It is a wild, untamed and instinctive form of expression which rejects the rules and norms established by the majority. A memory etched on the skin, it marks a date, a name, a place or an image, and fixes these emotive souvenirs for a lifetime. Above all, tattooing is the art of translating passion, and, because it often defies reason, it is condemned by the more wary in western civilisations.

On the other hand, tribal tattooing is readily accepted - for example, that which is still practised today by the Dayaks or Mentawi. Maybe this is because, as westerners, we don't feel involved in, or, more to the point, threatened by this form of tattooing?

14 This 1982 film tells how the beautiful Akane, with snow-white skin, was tattooed with the words "Pact with Death or with Fidelity" to please her lover. Throughout the film her pain is mixed with orgasm. The old master tattooist forces her to make love with his assistant as he drives the needles into her flesh. The assistant channels Akane's suffering according to the orders of his master. Each contraction from the impact of the needle tightens the embrace, until pain becomes inseparable from pleasure in this journey of initiation undertaken in silence.

15 Lenin bore the image of a skull on his chest, and Stalin a red star. Churchill was tattooed with the coat of arms of his ancestors, the Dukes of Marlborough and Montgomery displayed a butterfly on his forearm.

ETYMOLOGY

The word "tattoo" is probably of Polynesian origin. The natives of Polynesia use the word "tatau" to refer to the marks which they inscribe on their bodies. "Tatau" is most likely derived from "ta" (drawing) and "toua" (spirit), and indicates the role of the tattoo or "tatau" in providing a link with the afterworld, or the spiritual world. Some etymologists claim that the term is derived from the word "ta" (to beat), others that "tatau" (pronounced tattoo by the Polynesians) evolved from "tatatu" (to wound). Regardless of the accuracy of these various theories, it is clear that tattooing represented a hieroglyphical language which was widespread in this region, and which was interpreted by the tahowa - enlightened men.

In the culture of the South Sea Islands, as well as in the African and even Indian cultures, tattooing represents the culmination of a sacred process and is intended to express certain spiritual absolutes. The pain which it causes makes it more than a simple test: it affirms the courage of the person on whom it is bestowed. Those who try to avoid it are branded as cowards and banished. The tattoo represents a type of coat of arms obtained as a reward for patience and courage. The importance of its role is emphasised by its indelibility.

In Japan two words are used for tattoo, and the etymology of these two terms indicates the ambiguous nature of tattoo marks. The first word "irezumi" [16] is associated with the criminal world; the other, "horimono" [17] is used to refer to figurative tattoos which are applied voluntarily. During the Edo period [18] the devotees of the magnificent

panoramas inspired by Japanese engravings were concerned that they shouldn't be confused with criminals, and so took care not to tattoo their skin in those places where convicts' marks were usually branded: the face and the back of the arms. [19] This explains the typical "short suit" style of Japanese tattoos. With time, however, the distinction between the two terms became blurred until only the word "irezumi" was retained in common usage, thus endowing tattooing in Japan with an ominous double meaning.

The dictionary definition of tattooing is: "The method whereby animal or plant colourings are introduced under the epidermis to varying depths, producing a coloration or design, which, although not necessarily indelible, is extremely long-lasting." This definition does not refer to scarification, although it is achieved by the same process. The choice between the two methods is determined by skin colour. Scarification (incision producing a raised or sunken scar) sculpts dark skin, whereas tattooing is achieved by using contrasts on light-coloured skin.

Professor Darier, an acclaimed dermatologist, states that "tattooing refers to the marks or drawings produced by the voluntary introduction into the skin of insoluble, coloured particles, which remain there permanently."

The type of coloured particles used varies from country to country. China ink is the most universal, but lamp-black is easier to source. In the South Sea Islands it is obtained by burning the nut of the bancoulier [20] and mixing this with coconut oil and water. In Indonesia ashes are mixed with sugar cane juice, and, in Egypt, ashes are mixed with animal bile. A less exotic method of preparation is adopted in western prisons and barracks, where lamp-black is obtained from a spoon or the base of a pan which has been held over an open flame. In the old days, sailors would cover the drawings with a layer of gunpowder, and then set light to it. The subsequent explosion drove the powder particles deep into the skin. In Thailand the most commonly used colouring

16 The word "irezumi" comes from "ire," which means "to insert" and "zumi," which means "charcoal ink".

17 "Horimono" means "to engrave an object" or "to make an incision in an object."

18 Edo is the old name for Tokyo. The Edo era lasted from 1612 until 1867.

19 A dog tattooed on the forehead or two lines on the forearm indicated to all the gravity of the offence.

is indigo, which is obtained by dissolving crushed geckos. [21] The people of New Guinea use the sap of red leaves, and the Arabs of North Africa use pulverized antimony mixed with water melon and barley juice. Antimony also has the advantage of being antiseptic. In France, teenagers will use anything which comes to hand: pen ink, methylene blue, sulphur from matches, shoe polish, cocoa powder, crushed brick or slate - all mixed with saliva, or even urine!

Professional tattooists possess every conceivable colour in the form of mineral pigments with a base of iron oxide and titanium dioxide. Some are known to have allergenic properties: red contains cinnabar or mercury sulphur and green contains chrome oxide.

Although the method of injecting the pigment was perfected at the beginning of the century by Samuel O'Reilly's electric tattooing machine, the theory and techniques have hardly evolved at all since antiquity.

The sharp tool used varies according to local resources. The people of the Pacific islands use seashells, bird bones, fish bones, filed tortoiseshell or shark's teeth. If animal resources are in short supply, they are substituted by slivers of bamboo, cactus needles, nails, razor blades or shards of glass. The tool is mounted on a wooden handle, a piece of bamboo or cork, and struck with a mallet to pierce the skin and allow the pigment to penetrate. In the Maghreb, tattooing is carried out with a lancet called a mechalta, which is a steel instrument with a square, bevelled point that scarifies rather than pierces. As soon as blood is drawn, the tattooist injects the colourings into the wound. He might also add woman's milk which is supposed to provide strength......

There is much debate concerning the depth to which the colour penetrates the skin. A histological analysis of tattooed skin has shown that both the outer and inner layers of the skin are penetrated by the pigment. So it is obvious that any attempt to remove the tattoo will result in a conspicuous scar.

These technical details are supplemented by psychoanalytical information.

From the psychoanalytical point of view, tattooing is seen as an icon with the power to conceal - apparently allowing one to see everything, yet really hiding the essence.

Some people believe that these marks on the skin are an indication of the individual's instinctive quest for identity or equilibrium.

Both incision and decoration, tattooing is as close to the forms of mutilation practised by primitive cultures as it is to the forms of adornment adopted by our western civilisation; masks, clothing, make-up, which are merely coverings for the body .... its indelible, irrevocable character is the price which one pays.

20 The bancoulier is a tree from the euphorbiaceae family which grows in the Pacific islands. A rich, edible oil is extracted from its nuts.

21 Lizards are often kept as house pets in this region, as they are considered to have magical, protective qualities.

THE TA

TATTOOING: A PRIMITIVE RITUAL

"Man only exists by paying the price of demarcation, by which he determines and defines himself."
STAROBINSKI

If one were to give a nickname to this young Parisienne, it would probably be "Agile Feather." Her long hair and Navajo style jewellery complement the Indian tattoo, a symbol of independence. The indelible nature of the tattoo sets it apart from the other adornments: it has penetrated the barrier of the skin. The feathered earring adds the finishing touch to the subtle eroticism of this decorated shoulder.

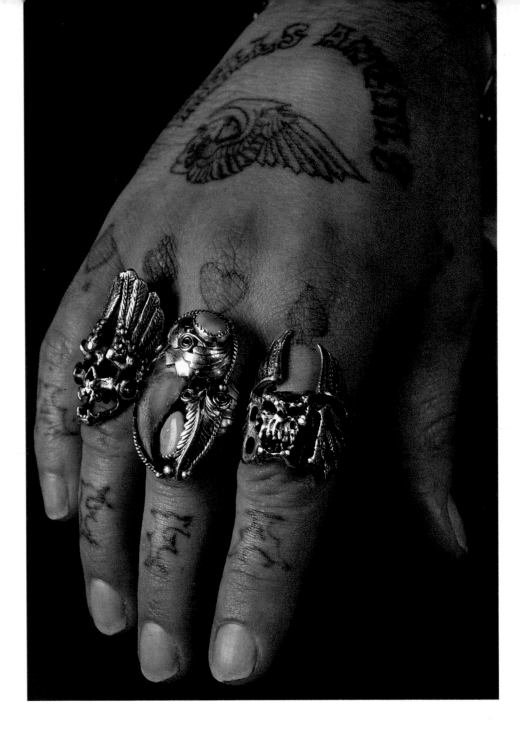

Left: The most persistent stereotype of the tattooed individual is that of the rebel on the fringes of society. Hell's Angels inscribe on their leather jackets and on their skin their collective insignia of a winged, helmeted skull. The "Angels" want to be branded for life to display their authenticity and commitment. AFFA stands for "Angels forever, forever Angels."

Right: Those who are tattooed are often following in the footsteps of primitive man, in that the mark is a social sign. Whereas, for primitive man, it represents integration in cultured society, in contemporary western society it represents voluntary exclusion from the prevailing culture. Distinguishing himself from the masses by means of the decorations on his body, the tattooed individual delves deep into the heart of ancient traditions in order to renew his links with a society which is closer to nature and provides a more optimistic outlook than the standardised uniformity of contemporary society. A scrap of black lace emphasises the curve of a feminine neckline, adding to its charm. A forearm doubles its power by wearing an engraved wristband similar to those of the Sarawak tribes in Malaysia.

Left: "Spiderman" Stephane sought inspiration from the Dayaks. He expresses very clearly his desire to progress from one state to another. The design he bears is intended to confirm this process of transcendence, fulfilling the same function as it would for members of primitive tribes. The shell of the Egyptian scarab, symbol of resurrection, is evident in this design. In Egyptian, the word for scarab comes from the verb "kheper," which means something along the lines of "to come to life by taking on a given form." The devotees of tribal tattooing consider it to be a sign of rebirth. It is also a sort of talisman. The colour black used in this type of tattooing is usually linked with death. Here, however, it confirms the transformation and emphasises that death is not an end in itself.

Right: The tattoo is a language which is engraved on the skin, making it more significant than clothes or other accessories which can be changed or removed. A type of magical vaccination, it represents an "inbuilt" mascot for its bearer. The motifs are often taken from comic strips. This design was inspired by Drulliet.

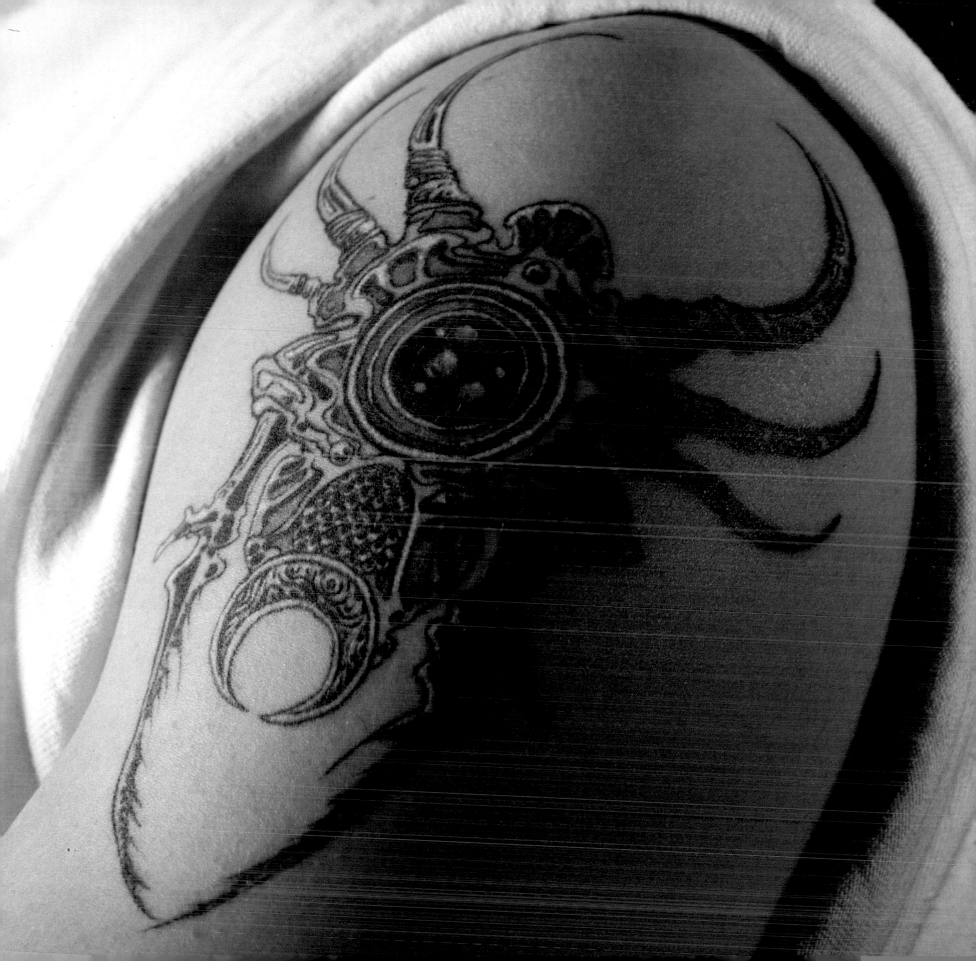

Tattooing is as much sculpture as it is painting and the tattooist plays with the contours of the anatomy........ In the bend of the elbow a dragon bares its teeth ferociously when the fist is clenched. The tattoo culminates in a design resembling a shirt cuff embroidered with Celtic knots.

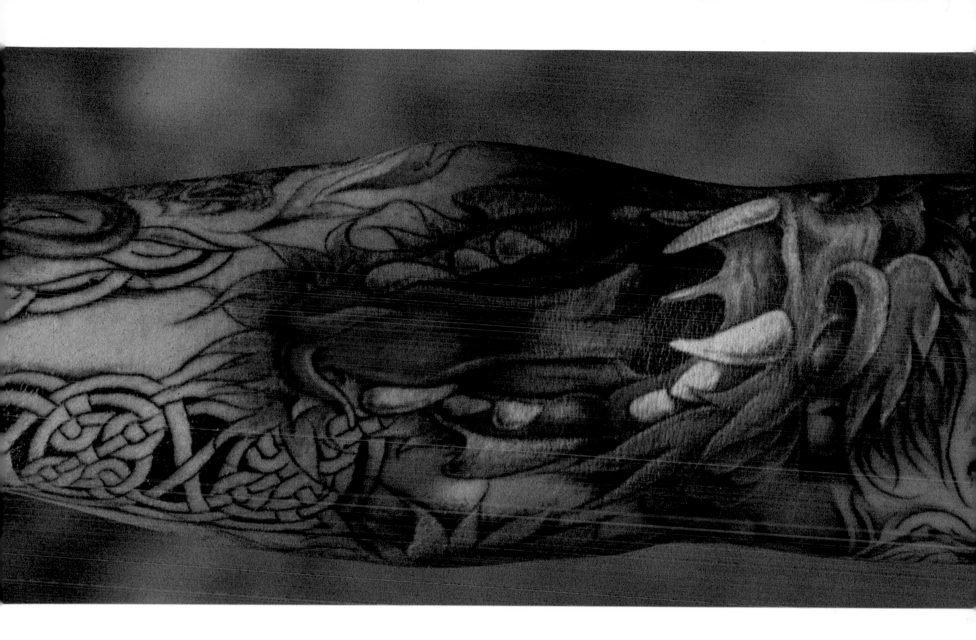

Left: A representation of death which is intended to be light-hearted and therefore liberating. Death is made into an object of mockery in order to calm the fear which it arouses. This man literally has death at his heels, but he doesn't care and just carries on enjoying life. Death is always present, whether it is lurking in the corner in its leering mask or represented in the form of an allegory. Here a cynical jester has words with a skull which is half clown, half skeleton.

Right: The ankle is a particularly painful part of the body to have tattooed. This circular tattoo symbolises the perpetual renewal of life. Here the circle form signifies a search for equilibrium and cosmic harmony. The red dragon, symbol of the masculine, represents strength and power. The green dragon, the feminine, holds the pearl, the Chinese emblem of wisdom.

The tattooed individual is often regarded as an exhibitionist with an urge to show off. Tattooing conventions provide him with the ideal opportunity to take the stage and win the admiration of those who are novices in the tattooing world and are eager to experience the extraordinary.

Left: Death and his henchmen rub shoulders with Christ crowned with thorns. This jolly trucker is a Harley-Davidson fanatic, who definitely has a "biker" look about him. Owner of a new, textured "identity card," which reinforces the feeling that he exists, the tattooed man crosses the boundaries of reality by glimpsing the dream beyond ....

Right: Which of these two opponents will be the victor - the macabre puppet, symbol of death, or the menacing tiger, symbol of power and virility?

Left: Film star or rock star? Everyone has their idol.... This cabling technician is a passionate fan of rock music.

Right: Those who are tattooed often reclothe themselves in the images of their heros, in the hope of capturing some of their super-human powers. Comic strips pro-vide ideal material for this type of tat-too. The iconogra-phy is easily repro-duced. Spiderman has the ability to extricate himself from the most diffi-cult situations and the person who bears his image in the form of a tattoo hopes to be endowed with simi-lar powers.

Left: "I forgot that your tattoos and your knife were, above all, an armour for your artichoke heart." Renaud in *Manu*.

Centre: The effect produced by tattooing is sometimes similar to that of the erotic clothes worn by women. Hair swept back, little black dress, black stockings and high heeled shoes are the classic contents of the erotic wardrobe...... Here the dress is cut away at the hip to reveal a baby leopard emerging from a bouquet of orchids.

Right: The tattoo is also a sign of recognition, an indication that the bearer belongs to a particular group - a group of initiates. So-called tribal tattooing is associated with the rituals of primitive tribes and represents a deliberate backward step - a return to the past, to man's roots. This former skinhead - since he has now adopted a different lifestyle - used to be the leader of a gang. He was possibly trying to indicate this by means of his moko style tattoo. In the Maori culture, tattooing is closely linked to social organisation, for this form of decoration was used to denote status and social rank. Only the Maori chiefs were permitted to have a facial tattoo. It was their signature.

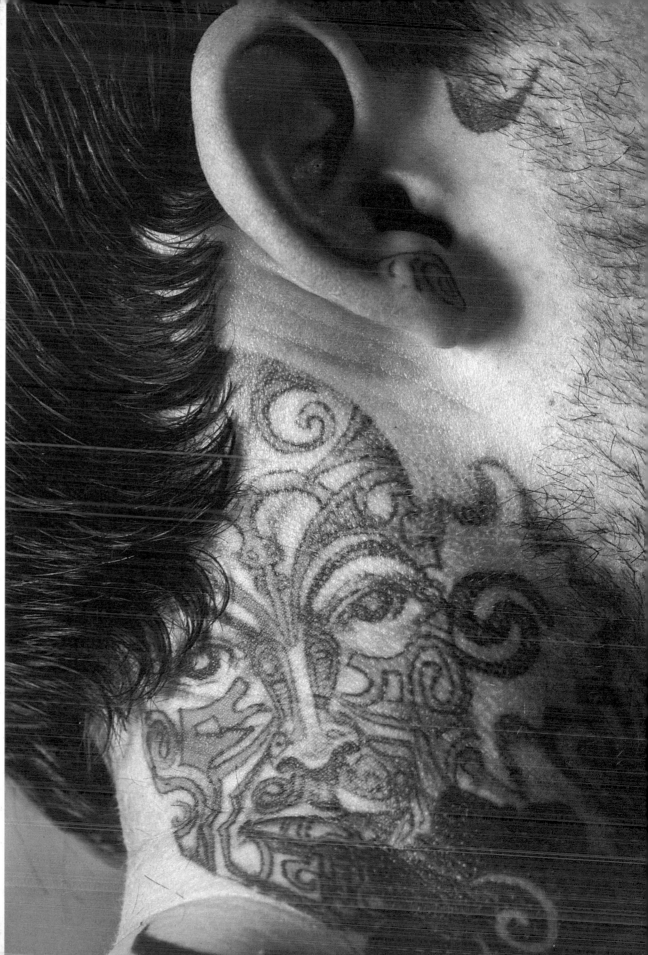

Left: A convict's chains and the Hell's Angels insignia - this image, designed and tattooed by the bearer, represents a cry for freedom.

Right: The tattooist has used the contours of the body's anatomy to produce the "skeleton" in this tattoo. The trunk follows the line of the spinal column, and the branches are shaped along the ribs. However this stylised tree does not represent the "tree of life." On the contrary it expresses the desolation of dying civilisations. On the right-hand side one can make out, through the branches, the characteristic visage of the Maori chiefs. A bare, dead tree struggling in the arid ground has been superimposed on the left-hand side. The only element of calm is the blue sky. It represents the desire to escape, the desire for the infinite, for purity, for another, more hospitable world. The precise composition of the design undoubtedly results more from a quest for harmony than from the desire to create an impressive decorative effect. The image is so strong that it must be significant.

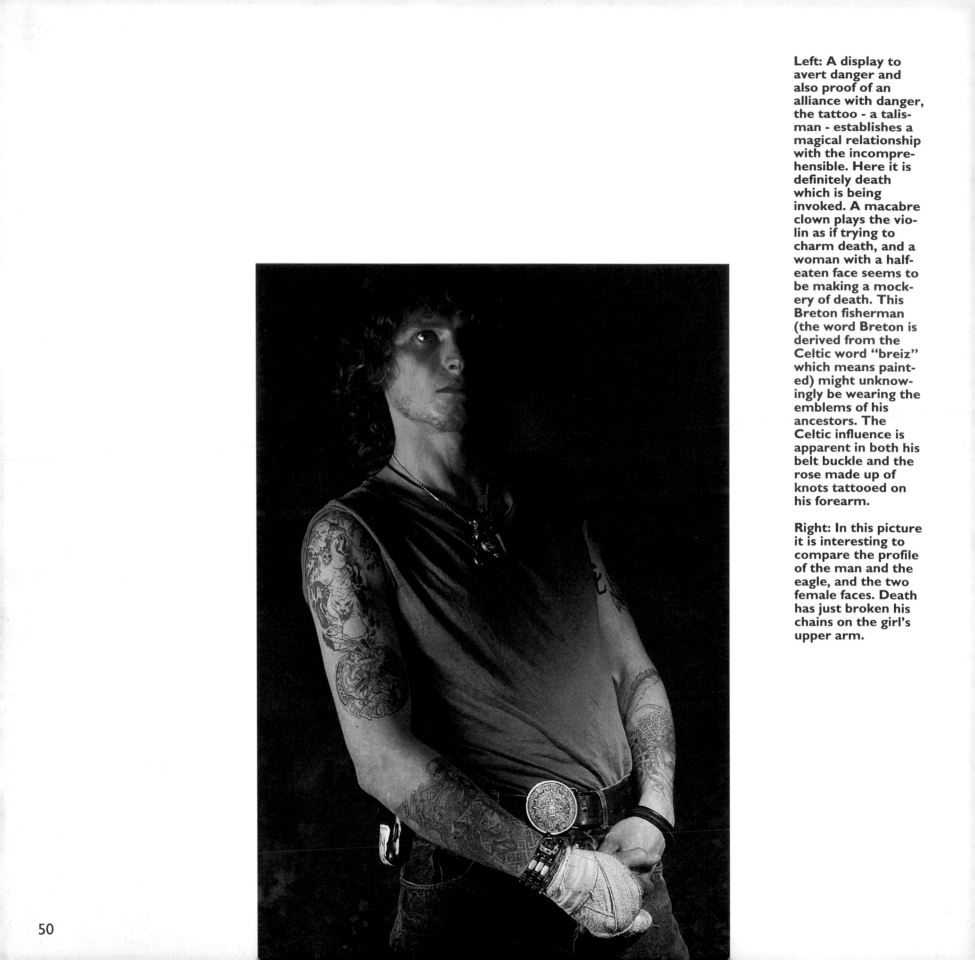

Left: A display to avert danger and also proof of an alliance with danger, the tattoo - a talisman - establishes a magical relationship with the incomprehensible. Here it is definitely death which is being invoked. A macabre clown plays the violin as if trying to charm death, and a woman with a half-eaten face seems to be making a mockery of death. This Breton fisherman (the word Breton is derived from the Celtic word "breiz" which means painted) might unknowingly be wearing the emblems of his ancestors. The Celtic influence is apparent in both his belt buckle and the rose made up of knots tattooed on his forearm.

Right: In this picture it is interesting to compare the profile of the man and the eagle, and the two female faces. Death has just broken his chains on the girl's upper arm.

Left: Who would guess that this sexy, young lady, a "piercing" enthusiast, is actually a Dutch nurse, who, in traditional style, wears a cap and a chastely buttoned white shirt for her job? The red hair and tattoos are a means of escape from a thoroughly conventional lifestyle. The tattoo on the right arm evokes the spirit of a dominant woman haunted by death.

Centre: An Italian tattooist displays his "biker" outfit. On his arm, Mario bears the insignia of his profession: a tattooing machine. The upper part of his body is covered with swirling spirals, like smoke rings. Spiralling into delightful thoughts? Soap bubbles which burst just like so many illusions?

Right: The theme of travel is clearly illustrated on this sailor. Souvenirs of Asia; the junk with saffron coloured sails (the colour of the Buddhist priests) and the snow covered summit of Mount Fujiyama are evocative images of the land of the rising sun. This volcano is a national monument in Japan, like the Eiffel Tower in France. Fujiyama means "the immortal" an ideal symbol to associate with tattooed skin.

Left: A zebra which looks as if it has been stencilled, and, on the chest, a beautiful image of Christ on the cross. The artist's signature is tattooed on the right breast like a stamp.

Right: Is it Satan himself who leads this group of monsters in a ritualistic dance? Is it the Minotaur who is leading submissive virgins to be sacrificed? The black colour and stylised design indicate the tribal origins of this tattoo. Maybe it relates to ancient rites?

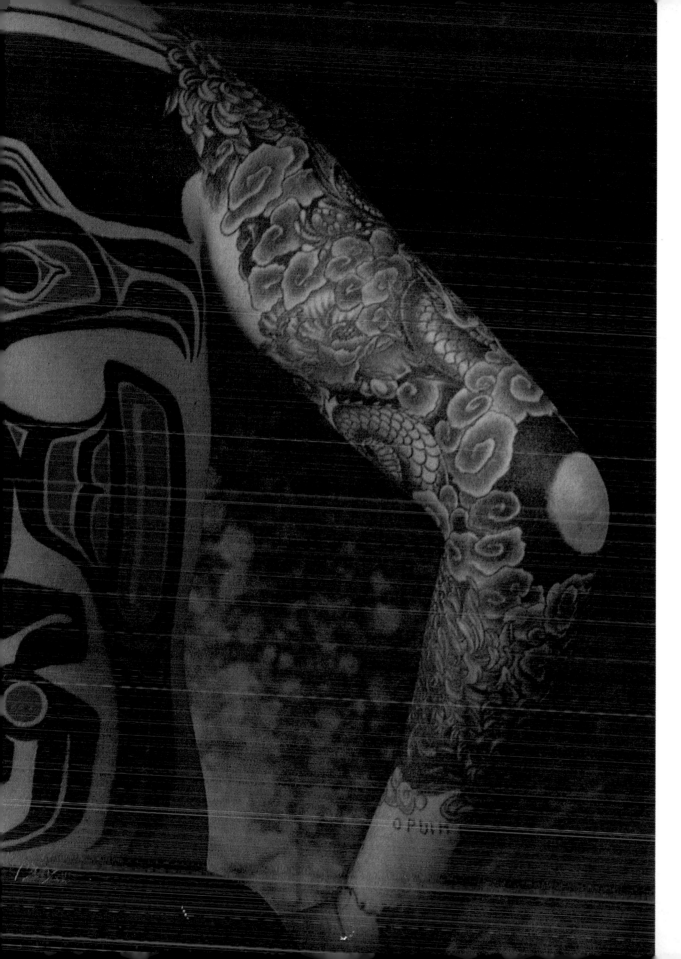

A typical Haïda (Canadian Indian tribe) spinal tattoo resembling a totem. Here the animal protector - totem - appears to be an eagle, symbol of power. The contrast between the colours red and black is indicative of the dichotomy between life and death. In contrast with the stark, black outlines - symbolising death - those parts of the design shaded in red symbolise the mystery of life which is concealed by dark shadows. It is the colour of the heart, of the womb. It represents the strength and power of cinnabar, but it can become a sign of death if it spills. Tattooing, a blood pact, unites the members of certain groups with life or with death.

Left: "Coco" is a real tiger! For this young, sensual, provocative South American tattooist the bloody inscription of the tattoo is part of the art of wounding and death.

Right: The instinct of the hunter bursts out in the form of a ferocious tiger, ready to pounce on its prey, having lacerated the skin. All its pent-up anger is unleashed. A cruel and merciless hunter, the tiger symbolises instinctive rage seeking appeasement. In traditional Chinese legends, the tiger is the opponent of the dragon, guardian of wisdom.

Left: This young Dutch woman was born in England and wanted to engrave in her flesh an indication of her profound attachment to the country of her birth. The British flag embraces the horn of plenty, a symbol of fertility and happiness, which is overflowing with flowers. Is the position of the tattoo on the most voluptuous part of her anatomy an invitation to the pleasures of the flesh? Small erotic tattoos are often strategically placed - on the breasts, buttocks, hips, top of the thighs - to attract the eye and focus feelings of desire....

Right: A macabre portrait of Merlin the wizard, holding a tattooing machine in his claw-like hands. Two bony hands, clasped as if in prayer, emerge from the molten lava in the cauldron. Does this vision of hell depict the fate of those who are tattooed?

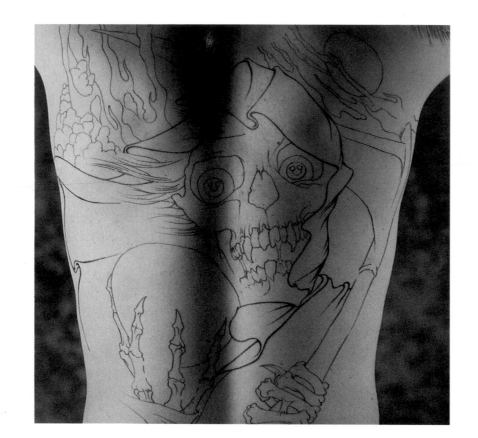

Left: Tattooing in progress. Death is always lurking, for those who are tattooed belong to the group which denounces it as the ultimate scandal. This Leviathan, armed with a sickle and a crystal ball should be adorned with swastikas - symbols of eternity. This tattoo is the result of close collaboration between the tattooist and the customer, a joint piece of work, in which each of the pair is evoking his own personal vision of the theme. The customer insists that it should be unique. He has been visiting the tattooist twice a week for six months in order to draft the outline of the design on his back. The tattooist, who is more familiar with symbolic interpretation, has suggested that the clothing in the tattoo should be decorated with swastikas, which, apart from their symbolic connotations, are also a flexible graphical form.

Centre: This saint apostle, in the process of giving his blessing, resembles an icon with his rigid, lifeless stance.

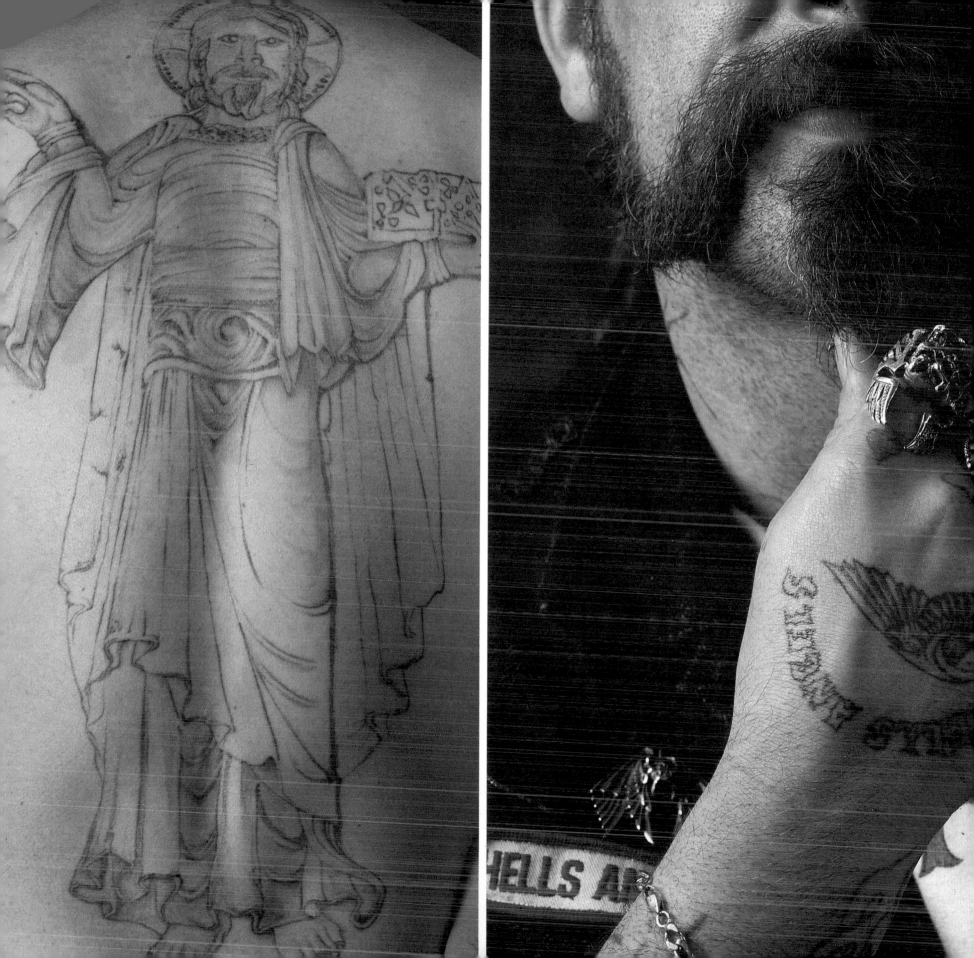

This couple of senior executives have the same tastes and enjoy the same things. Because they do everything together, they decided to have similar motifs tattooed in the same places on each of their bodies as a sign of their mutual love and fidelity. The resulting tattoos are a mixture of tribal and figurative designs.

The skull of a bull surrounded by feathers signifies death for the American Indians. According to Jung's analysis of symbolism, the sacrifice of a bull represents "the desire for a spiritual life which would enable man to transcend his primitive animal instincts, and which, after an initiation ceremony, would bring him peace." The sacrificial symbolism is reinforced by the feathers. Man has killed the beast which sleeps within him, and the feathers are proof of the sacrificial undertaking. Every aspect of this man indicates his affinity with Indian culture: the braided hair, the jewellery from Nevada.....

TRIBAL TATTOOS

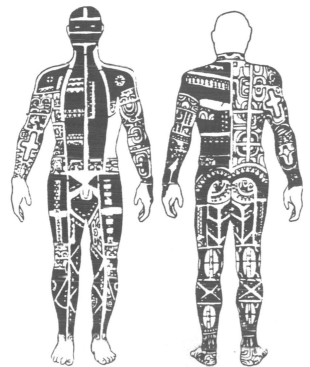

Tattooing symbolises the transition from one state of being to another. It bestows a socio-cultural identity on the individual who suffers to acquire it. A sign of status in all primitive tribes, it is still regarded as a sign of marginal groups in western countries.

Is it a coincidence that, both in 20th century Europe and in the primitive societies of the Pacific islands, the first experience of tattooing is usually acquired in adolescence?

The adolescent is at a transitional stage, an important crossroads in his life, and he is fascinated by the adult world and its promise of knowledge. But he hesitates to relinquish the innocence of his childhood world.

In primitive tribes, this transition from childhood to adulthood is marked by a ritual. The protocol of the ritual, passed down from one generation to the next, is a law which must be obeyed without question. When he reaches a certain age, the child becomes a man by way of an initiation ceremony which is intended to challenge and test him.

This transformation is validated by the traditional stamp of a tattoo or scarification, which represents the key part of the initiation rite. This stamp on the skin documents life's milestones in the same way as our certificates of birth, marriage and death. In the absence of written records, the people of these tribes wear on their skin the marks which indicate their social and family status. One glance is enough to ascertain the place of birth, tribe of origin, battle exploits, marital status and sometimes even medical history. This form of tattooing really is a type of coded language.

In the Maori tribes of New Zealand, tattooing of the face, a sign of power and authority, is restricted to the chiefs. Each unique design is called a moko. This seal is the equivalent of a coat of arms.

The Iban head-hunters of Borneo proudly display their bravery by tattooing the number of decapitations which they have performed on the back of their hands.

The Sarawak women, who maintain a longstanding tradition of weaving and plaiting, tattoo the qualifications of their ability on their forearms. Without this certificate of qualification, they would be unlikely to receive any proposals of marriage.

These tribal tattoos are a sign of maturity, male virility and female charm, and are also a testimony to courage, since the pain involved has to be borne in silence to retain self-esteem.

This stamp is more than a sign of recognition and symbol of integration into the tribe - it is a type of baptism, which seals the new identity.

When the young man arrives at the tattooing ceremony, he is both proud and frightened, but, above all, he understands the reasons why this needs to be done. The tribal rites impose this mark upon him to strike fear into his enemies, to seduce women and to promote him to the ranks of the initiated - in short, to make him a man.

The mystical-religious rite of tribal tattooing represents a symbolic death followed by rebirth. It provides the individual with access to another world, outside the plane of reality.

A label of authenticity

In western society, the teenager, trapped in a sort of ageless limbo, tries to get himself noticed by doing crazy things. If he tattoos his skin, it is as much a type of armour as it is decoration. It is also to show that he exists. In our society there is no ceremony to mark the change in status. It is merely a case of reaching an age which brings with it certain rights, and this happens anonymously, recorded only by a piece of paper. In contrast to the practices of primitive tribes, in western society the teenager is alone during this testing time, facing the adult world, which is both appealing and frightening. Some are able to pass through this period without any problems, others, however, need some sort of a compass and the tattoo can fulfil this role.

Tattooing marks this transformation. Because of the pain associated with it, tattooing gives the impression of belonging to the adult world. But its expression remains childlike. The dedication "a thought for my mother" can turn into the rebellious "death to the cops," a beast or the hero of a comic strip, admired for his invincible strength..... It is a cry which tears the skin, whilst building a barrier to protect it.

The youths who tattoo their skin do so because they want to be decorated, coloured and, more important, labelled for life, stamped to prove their authenticity.

Thus they make their mark not only with clothes and make-up, but also by crossing the barrier of the skin. Whereas clothes and make-up can be removed without consequence, the removal of a tattoo leaves permanent scars.

The indelibility of the tattoo provides reassurance, in that it doubles the thickness of the skin. Both a cry and an affirmation of existence, it objectifies feelings of misery in order to liberate the individual from them. It is an irrefutable proof of passage to emancipated status. The adolescent becomes "a real man, a tattooed man" as in the words of Mistinguett's song. He looks tough and hard, and bears proof of his courage in his resistance to self-inflicted pain, which justifies the price of transcendence. The pain, which is feared, but can also be an erotic experience, is essential. To the observer it can appear absurd and gratuitous. However it is an inherent part of the metamorphosis. It makes one aware of the wound. Isn't it the case that suffering for no other reason than to want to bear the pain represents a victory over one's own nature?

In conclusion, the tattooed westerner undergoes a process which is similar to that of primitive man, but with the opposite aim in mind. The primitive man is trying to raise himself from the basic animal level. Tattoos are his means of access to civilisation and they elevate him to human status. His contemporary western counterpart however is denying civilisation. His body decorations are a sign of his desire to commune with all that is wild and natural. He plumbs the depths of ancient traditions and gains strength by rediscovering the more simple values.

Challenging conventions

A mark for eternity, the tattoo is also the expression of a deliberate, if brief act of will. By means of tattoos, the individual sets himself apart from the society which he has rejected and places himself firmly on the margin.

The sophisticated media of the 20th century tends to unify attitudes by means of mass communication. The tattooed individual tries to remain on the outside of this uniformity. In an attempt to give meaning to his own existence, he forages through his past in search of his roots and his own personal truths. He navigates back up the stream of time to renew his ties with nature, unite with the cosmos and gain the sensation of being at one with the Whole. The current fascination with tribal tattoos reflects this desire to return to our roots. This type of adornment gives the tattooed individual the feeling of being unique in an anonymous and standardised world. He distinguishes himself by changing his skin - restructures himself.

This "coat of arms" is also a challenge - to adults, to conventions, to the system.

In a world where ideologies are dying and families are breaking up, tattooed people are creating groups of initiates with their own rules and values. This return to the tribal clan system appears to be a quest for the lost meaning of life. This community provides support, care and reassurance, similar to that received from a mother figure. It renews family feeling and offers an alternative way of life, which, if one enters into it, can be like a form of rebirth.

Even though the rebellious adolescent might think of himself as an adult, and wants to stand on his own two feet, deep down he really has a need to go back to a protective cocoon. So he escapes from his family, where he feels smothered and misunderstood, and joins the "gang," where familial ties are

replaced by human warmth. Tattooing becomes a sign of recognition and returns a lost identity. It fulfils the initiation role, as in primitive societies, and unifies the members of the same clan. Tattooing also enables the individual to substitute his own identity with the more reassuring group identity.

In search of the supernatural

Tattooed people often search for their roots amongst the most remote and primitive civilisations of the Pacific islands, who are clearly distanced in all respects from the orderly, organised, so-called civilised world. However, Indian and Celtic motifs are on the increase in the current iconography. This is not a coincidence. The primitive tribes of the Pacific, the American Indians and the Celts all have the same philosophy. Their line of thought is cosmic, mystical, taking them beyond the boundaries of reality. They all live in the world of ideas. They are not prisoners of a social system - the gods are the arbiters of their affairs. They establish "magical," paralogistical societies, which are less formalistic and materialistic than our own. It is easy to understand the attraction which this lifestyle holds for the dreamer, in particular the idealistic teenager.

Tattooing a Sioux or a Comanche on one's back - isn't this a way of demonstrating that one is an independent spirit, just like those free and proud races?

The Indian nomad, who is generally misunderstood - particularly by the white people - and is constantly rebelling against organised society, provides an ideal role model for our young rebels. He also evokes childhood memories of cowboy and indian fights, western epics which have provided endless material for films and comic strips. This return to Indian culture represents the search for a lost paradise, where freedom and harmony reign. It expresses the desire to belong to a well-defined race with its rites and legends, and a lifestyle so different from our contemporary consumer society.

Is there a link between these "western tattoos" and the poetic Indian nicknames which are derived from the totem?

Names such as "Lynx Eye," Agile Panther" or "Spirited Horse" are intended to evoke the main characteristics of their bearers, and, when tattooed on the back or the chest, they build a bridge between two worlds.

As for the "Celtic tattoo" with its entwined braids and knots emblazoned on the chest like feudal armour - doesn't it represent the never-ending quest for the Holy Grail? Is it merely a fashion fad, or is it a coded expression of the search for noble, spiritual values similar to those of the feudal knights?

In Celtic art - and especially in Irish designs - the knots which are always present symbolise endless motion. They are a labyrinth through which one travels in search of the centre (resolution and release), which holds the promise of serenity and inner contentment if it can be reached. The knots represent the twists of fate. In spiritual terms, untying the knots symbolises the liberation of the self from bonds and the freedom to live on a more elevated plane.

Does the tattooist, endlessly embroidering intertwined cords and figures-of-eight, regard himself as one of the Fates, knotting the threads of existence? Does he offer access to enlightenment and immortality to those who, marked by the symbol, are guided by it along the path they have to tread?

Even though the institution of knighthood, which originated from the legend of King Arthur, died out a long time ago, the concept of the knight still persists. From medieval to modern literature, including comic strips, the ideal of knighthood is expressed in symbolic form, as an essentially virtuous character, who loyally lives his life according to a certain code of beliefs and commitments. The knight is a servant, an eternal suitor for his Lady (the idealised woman) and, like Percival, a participant in the quest for the Holy Grail. He frequently resorts to violent methods to pursue his elevated, spiritual goal, but his battles are always in a noble cause. Violent and impetuous, the knight is far from being the ideal man without any weaknesses - which makes him more human- but he is loyal and courageous, a man of honour, who is never tainted by the corruption and crime which surround him. This type of code is also found, curiously enough, in contemporary organised gangs, many of which are considered to be outlaws and delinquents. The Hell's Angels are an example. Honour is their main priority, even if it necessitates violence. They are not afraid to display their affiliation to the group on their leather jackets and their skin. The winged helmet with the number "I", the mark of their motorcycle, a superb Harley-Davidson, their rank, their rally point, even their nicknames - everything is engraved.

This return to the past can appear regressive to westerners, who find it hard to grasp the desire to return to an uncivilised state. In fact it is a search for roots, a return to original sources. Isn't an escape to the irrational the ultimate method of evading the uniformity of urban society, where the obligation to produce or consume is paramount? In returning to the heart of humanity and reviving ancient practices, does the tattooed person feel as if he has been reborn?

TALISMAN TATTOOING

"One had to be painted to be a man. Those who didn't alter their natural state were indistinguishable from the animals."
CLAUDE LEVI-STRAUSS

In addition to its symbolic value as a coat of arms or a medal, the tattoo also has sacred connotations. The role which it plays in ritual procedures is loaded with spiritual and supernatural implications.

The tattoo enables the individual to lift his body out of the banality of the everyday, and to make it a cult object.

Throughout his life the initiate bears the indelible mark of this sacred ritual, which differentiates him from the non-initiates.

In primitive tribes, tattooing and scarification record irrevocable events or situations which have been resolved once and for all, such as coming of age, marriage, wars, deaths.

In these tribes, painting merely expresses a transitory state of mind. Jubilation is indicated in decorations which are vivid and bright - faces painted in white, ochre and red and coloured feathers, leaves and seashells in the hair. During tribal wars, the decorations are modified to communicate ferocity, aggression and strength. The men use charcoal to paint their bodies black. They abandon the bright leaves which symbolise health and well-being and replace them with the dull, grey leaves usually reserved for mourning. They substitute the colourful feathers with those from birds which are supposed to be an ill omen for their enemies.

Painting, which is not a bloody or painful process, does not leave any traces. As soon as the celebration is over, the paint is washed off. Whereas tattooing is both painful - since it involves injecting a foreign substance into one's body - and definitive. It allows access to the sublime and, ultimately, to transfiguration.

The power of the flesh

These tribal rituals are the equivalent of a second creation, where the initiate is reborn in the totem [22] - the sacred, mythical ancestor of the tribe. It is believed that, during this rebirthing process, the initiate takes on some of the powers of the totem.

The representation of the totem on the bodies, clothing and ritual objects of the tribe is intended to show the cohesion and strength of the tribe.

People are always searching for a mythical figure to worship. Teenagers cover the walls of their rooms with pictures of their idols, wear T-shirts and badges adorned with them, and try to look like them. One might even conclude that, in tattooing names and faces onto his body, the teenager is trying to transcend his own personality in order to identify completely with his idol.

The flesh thus exposed, cut, perforated and illuminated is invested with power and crosses the boundaries of reality.

Therefore, from the primitive tribes of the South Seas to the Celts, from the American Indians to westerners, the goal has always been the same - for the human condition to transcend nature on an everlasting basis.

A blood pact

The tribute of blood makes tattooing into a sacrifice. It takes courage to let blood flow. The fellowship represented by this blood is highly symbolic in all cultures. In 5 BC, the Scythians would conclude their alliance treaties by making incisions on their bodies. The blood which flowed as a result was collected and mixed with wine in a cup, from which all the signatories of the treaty would drink as a pledge of eternal friendship and support. Similarly, Christ and the apostles shared the symbolic blood at the Last Supper. This ritual has been maintained in the form of Communion. For the ancient Greeks and the Aztecs the sacrifice of blood was an offering to the gods. In the Middle Ages, soldiers would enter into blood pacts with each other. The knights were united in a friendship which they would not even dishonour for the woman they loved. For the gypsies, the exchange of blood signifies an exchange of love and eternal loyalty, which can only be ended by death. Their marriages, or, sometimes, friendships are sealed by cuts made on the wrist. For Africans,

22 The totem represents the mythical and sacred ancestor of the tribe or clan, and is supposed to bring prosperity, energy and power to the group.

this exchange of blood indicates the most serious form of friendship. Entered into voluntarily by both parties, this fellowship takes precedence over any biological or physiological bonds. The people of Papua, New Guinea slash their arms and those of their visitors with a sharp bamboo stick as a sign of peace. Secret societies, gangs and sects also practise this type of alliance. The famous Yakusa in Japan can be identified by their panoramic tattoos and their amputated fifth finger - signs of their power and determination.

Blood, a symbol of life, has a magic meaning and therefore an esoteric quality. Whether it is a question of a simple incision or a tattoo, the goal is the same: to ensure complicity by sharing that which is most precious and vital. To break a blood pact is to condemn oneself to death.

A magic precaution

Like a vaccination, the tattoo also offered protection against occult forces, without any direct engagement on the part of its bearer. The amulet and the charm have always been practical intermediaries between man and the gods.

The unusual or unfamiliar always provokes a profound insecurity in man, due to the fragility of the human condition. In the same way as primitive man fears anything which cannot be subjected to tribal rules and establishes a taboo for that which appears abnormal, his contemporary is suspicious of anything which he does not understand or with which he is unfamiliar. Some people protect themselves against misfortune by prayer, supplication and religious medallions to "chase away the demons." Others rely on tattooing to evade evil, banish the idea of death and negate the potentially catastrophic effects of the unknown.

It is like a narcissistic challenge to death. Existential dread is always there, skin deep. Everyone lives with it, plays tricks with it, expresses it in their own way. Just as the soul is immortal for believers, the tattoo can be made immortal, for one can bequeath one's skin. Death is always there in a corner of the picture, a grimacing, foolish clown mask, a simple skull, a skeleton armed with a scythe or personifications of Leviathan or Beelzebub. The hounds of Satan sneer and dance their macabre waltz on man's skin. Who will finally win the skins of the others?

In some countries even the ink has a special composition in order to achieve a beneficial effect. In Thailand, for example, it is mixed with pulverized lizard skin or bull's bile.

A true talisman, the tattoo is a passport for the afterworld.

In primitive tribes, tattooing is the gateway to the taboo domain of the next world. It opens up contact with the celestial powers by changing the essence of man. He must modify his appearance and adorn himself with symbols to effect his magical transformation and allow him to communicate with the deities. Embellishment in the literal sense of the word is not the goal. Man must deface himself, go beyond his natural form, betray his anatomy to become inhuman and to facilitate "the journey."

The next world - heaven, hell or nirvana - is the "absolute other." There the gods appear quite different to man, far removed from the images and the sublimation which are familiar to us in our civilisation. The Dayaks believe that their tattoos provide a resistance to bodily decay and a means of recognition in the next world. According to them, the future life lies in a mythical place, where everything is the opposite to this world. Therefore, based on this belief, the members of this tribe tattoo themselves in dark colours so as to be visible in the land of shadows. These tattoos consist of stylised figures outlined in bold, thick lines, conspicuous enough to exceed the limits of the terrestrial world. On the contrary, in our western Judeo-Christian civilisation, God has been conceived in the image of man. He is the Father and represents the ultimate sanctuary when confronted with the hostility of nature or acute existential dread. Man does not have to, and, indeed, should not modify his appearance to come

closer to God. In fact, the eternal Father, born in Christ, shows himself to be a simple mortal, on a human scale.

Thus it is difficult for Christians to recognise tattooed individuals as brothers. These men and women look like us, but their coloured bodies alienate them from us, as if they are either too close or too remote for comfort. In the collective consciousness they are often grouped together with savage hordes of head-hunters and other hybrid beings - neither man nor beast. So they arouse fear. Excluded from our well-organised world these tattooed people evolve along a parallel path, to which only the initiates can gain access.

Why not take a short cut and change planets for a moment, just to see? Why not abandon this ambiguous, uneasy feeling and allow yourself to be led to the other side of the mirror?

THE TATTOO:
A PERMANENT
ORNAMENT

"The concept of an ideal torments even the most primitive nature. The savage who tattoos and paints himself with red or blue and pierces his nose with a fish bone has a confused idea of beauty. He is searching for something beyond what he is. He tries to perfect himself, guided by an obscure notion of art."
THÉOPHILE GAUTHIER

A friendly, photogenic "Buddha." A monster is trying to make its way out of his stomach. Maybe because it is suffocating? This tattooist started amassing his own collection of tattoos while he was still at school. Having developed a passion for tattooing, he continued to cover himself with designs in a rather haphazard way, dotting them randomly all over his body.

Left: A skinhead trying to be provocative. Punk style launches a deliberate attack on the humanist image of the body. The punks adopted as their totems the emblems of a "techno-fascist" tribalism. By distorting their body image, they anticipate biological degradations. "No Future" and "Hate and War" are their slogans. In a light-hearted yet self-destructive manner they try to draw attention to themselves and to inspire horror.

Right: This woman has a permanent, although somewhat outdated covering of underwear..... The fine, flowery bolero with embroidered sleeves clashes with the crazy array of beasts tattooed below her waist. No doubt the soft, romantic top half is intended to reflect a tender heart, whereas the lower part suggests a sultry, burning character. Even the devil sticks out his tongue towards this fiery sex. Margaret is glad to show her tattoos to anyone who makes a polite request......

Left: An unusual series of reproductions - true "transfer mania" - which juxtaposes a laughing rat perched on a skull, a marijuana leaf, an urchin, a skull in a top hat holding a rose between its teeth - making an extravagant creation into something resembling a joke.

Right: The tattoo isolates and transforms certain areas of anatomy. Here the breast is a rock surrounded by breaking waves. The position of the tattoo is as evocative as the motif itself. Womens' tattoos almost always have erotic connotations. Because it is hidden, the tattoo is a "part of the self" concealed from the gaze of others and reserved for the privileged.

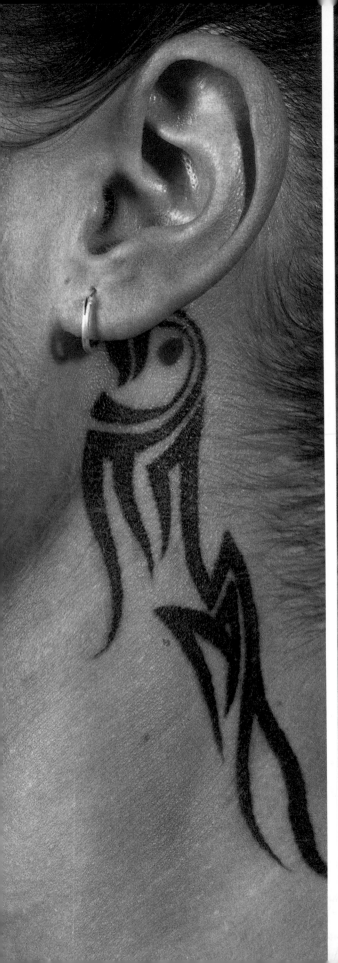

Left: When it is exposed to view, the tattoo can function in the same way as a piece of jewellery. This design extends the earring in a smooth, flowing motion, so that it resembles a dangling pendant in rythm with the steps of the person wearing it.

Centre: These permanent stockings draw the eye further and further up the thighs towards the octopus which is caressing them.

Right: This American tattooist, Peggi, presents the perfect example of Japanese ornamental tattooing. She has turned her body into a real jewel. The design of this tattoo incorporates the principal symbols of longevity: the dragon, the chrysanthemum and the carp. The chrysanthemum represents plenitude and the maturity of an autumn flower. The carp brings good luck and is a symbol of both material and spiritual fertility, due to its reputation for prolific reproduction. It is also an embodiment of courage and perseverance, as its life cycle involves a plucky and arduous struggle to swim upstream against the river current.

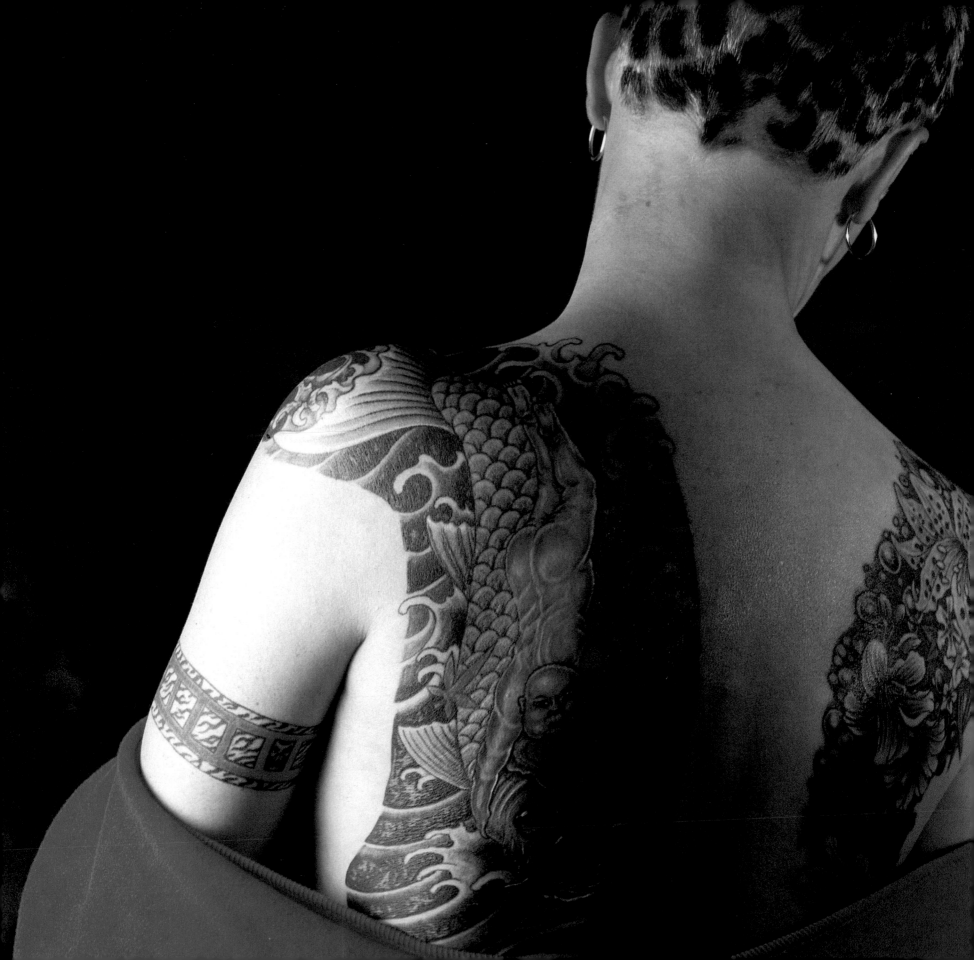

Left: The body, never truly naked, is clothed in a second skin. Tattooing provides it with an extravagant costume, or, in this case, a small waistcoat to keep the shoulders warm. This is a depiction of the legend of Kintaro, a classic theme in Japanese iconography. Sonja is a therapist. She succumbed to temptation and had a small tattoo done during a convention in Amsterdam in 1987. After that she became hooked and gradually added more and more decorations, always careful to observe the aesthetic qualities of the design. Her tattoos are easily concealed by her clothes, and she had them done purely for her own pleasure, because she enjoys looking at them in the mirror.

Right: A detail from a Japanese tattoo: the pearl is the symbol of yin, the feminine. At a more mystical level, it represents enlightenment and wisdom. The dragon guards this treasure, the key to wisdom.

Left: For men the tattoo is a symbol of virility, as it was necessary to suffer to earn it. The iconography contains abundant symbols of power and aggression, such as the tiger or the eagle. The element of domination is emphasised in this design by the quasi-human head with a gaping mouth which has torn its way through the chest.

Right: A living legend, the tattoo is a true fresco engraved on the skin. This story was taken from an English comic strip which recounts the exploits of the Celtic warrior, Slane. The quality of the design and the complicated colour tones elevate this picture to the level of masterpiece. This tattoo has won many awards: after being awarded 3rd prize in the USA in 1990, it won the 1st prize at an international convention in Paris in 1991.

Left: This young German was asked if the tattoos on his face posed any problem in his relationships with his colleagues at the brewery where he works. "People are a bit surprised at first, then they get used to it when they get to know me." Nevertheless facial tattoos can prove troublesome in everyday life, as they are an overt sign of rebellion. In addition to the tattoos on his face, this man bears a self-portrait on his breast showing his appearance before and after tattooing - a sort of photographic souvenir - and, on his ear, the Freemason's eye.

Right: The tattooed woman is disturbing. She distances her body in order to make it into an exhibit. Feline, bewitching, she is a match for the toughest man. This beautiful Danish woman from Copenhagen is completely covered in tattoos, and is also keen on piercing - ears, lower lip, nose, nails, nipples.

Left: This tattoo, created free-hand by Jo Marina, has a strong Japanese theme. Many people who have been tattooed turn to renowned artists to modify bungled tattoos from their adolescence which they regret having done. Others go to the doctor to pay the price of the sins of their youth - the price being an ugly scar. This tattoo was created from an existing design. The dragons symbolise the conflict between two opposing yet complementary principles: the struggle between reason and instinct. They represent the neutralising of adverse tendencies: sulphur, or the active principle, yang, reacts with mercury, or the inert principle, yin, to form cinnabar. It is said that this alchemic mixture can bestow immortality. What is more certain, however, is that cinnabar - the base of the red colour used by tattooists - causes the most extreme allergies.

Right: Hiroshima mon amour! Usually one starts with a small, discreet tattoo, like a piece of jewellery. Then, often, visits to various conventions lead to a sort of "tattoo mania" until the whole body is reclothed .....

A figurative depiction of an iguana on the left, and a more stylised version in the centre. The interaction between tattoos, clothing and accessories is like a game. Tattoos are usually located in areas which can be covered or uncovered at will. It is clear that leather clothes are fundamental garments in the tattooed person's wardrobe. Is this because they evoke the softness of the skin, and, like tattoos, offer the extra protection of an added skin?

Right: Is this a modern day knight in his chain mail of tattoos? His chiselled armour is welded to the contours of his muscles, with a little bit of give at the elbows. It covers the whole body. The helmet with ram's horns on the shoulder is a symbol of virile power and is typically Celtic. In classic iconography the Gauls wore horned helmets.

Left: Another tattoo with a Japanese feel to it. The chrysanthemum - the national flower - and the famous breaking wave of Hokusai are particularly prominent.

Right: A magnificent pectoral tattoo inspired by Celtic designs. It features the two emblems of the knights of the Round Table. The dog, a loyal companion, is the symbol of gallantry and the young woman represents the feminine ideal, pure and chaste. Her long, flowing hair is a sign of her nobility and availability. The stylised elements of the background - the knotted and braided threads - are typical of Pict art and symbolise the fundamental link. The noble knight is linked to his lady and his dog forever.

Arabesque pattern. Even the hands are tattooed.

Anatomy can accommodate any fantasy..... The elbow is a mainstay for lively designs: a flower in bloom, a spider weaving its web, the gaping jaws of a monster, a dragon leaping into life, and a long-sleeved cardigan which appears to have worn into a hole at the elbow.....

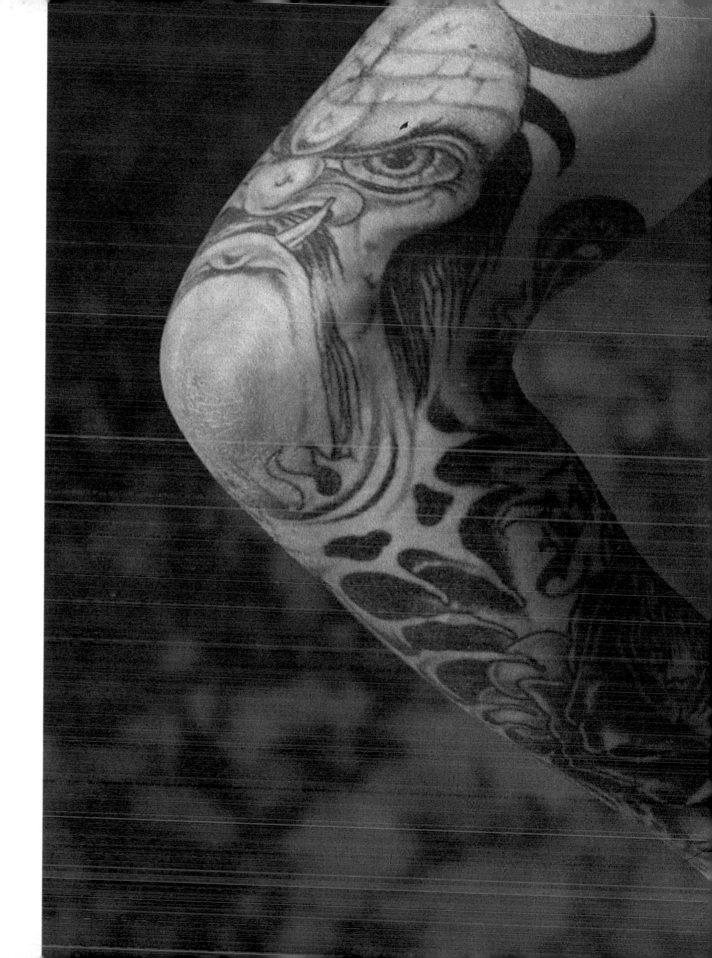

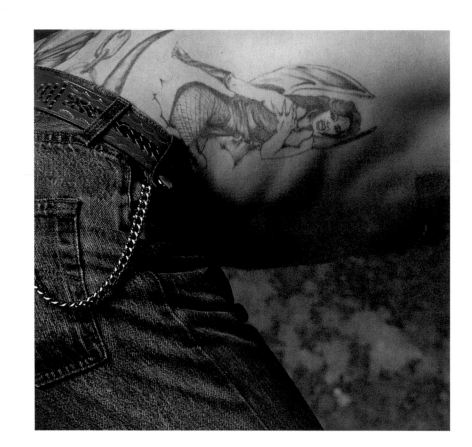

Left: A provocative young woman pops up out of this man's belt like a jack-in-the-box. An invitation to pleasure?

Right: Just as women use their tattoos as an erotic tool in the seduction process, for men, tattoos are a means of expressing their sexual fantasies - the streetwalker being a particularly popular motif.

Raised in a family with a long-standing tradition of tattooing, this English tattooist was fifteen when he acquired his first tattoos, a panther and a snake. His father is completely covered in tattoos. He saw it as a natural progression to emulate his father, and each year he adds new designs to his diverse array of symbols. The most noteworthy motifs in his random collection are the dedication to his mother **"MUM,"** the yin/yang symbol and the terrifying mask tattooed on his neck, providing him with a second, more horrifying face.

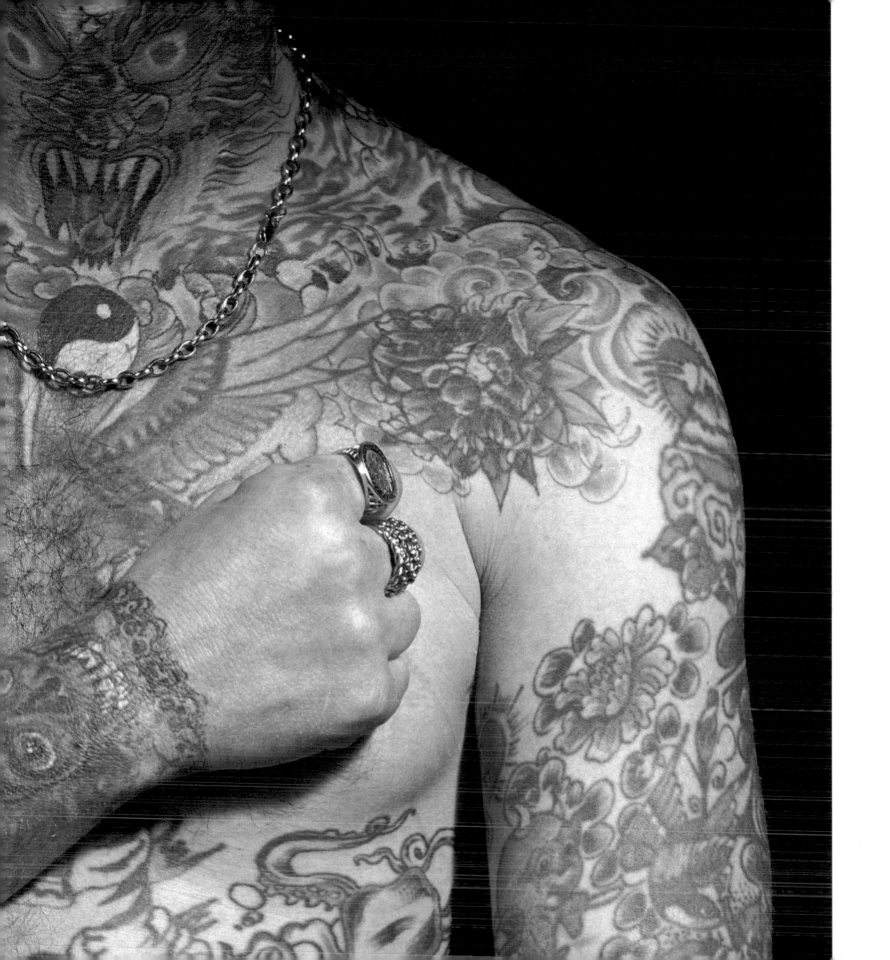

Left: The stereotype of the tattooed individual is usually some sort of rebellious teenager or someone on the fringe of society who wants to be different from the rest and displays his rejection of the system. Tattoos, wild hairstyles, bizarre accessories, such as a rat's foot earring, are deliberately worn to shock.

Right: Tattooing is an ideal medium for expressing sexual fantasies of domination and submission. Sexual impulses are externalised in order to control them and openly displayed in order to exorcise them.

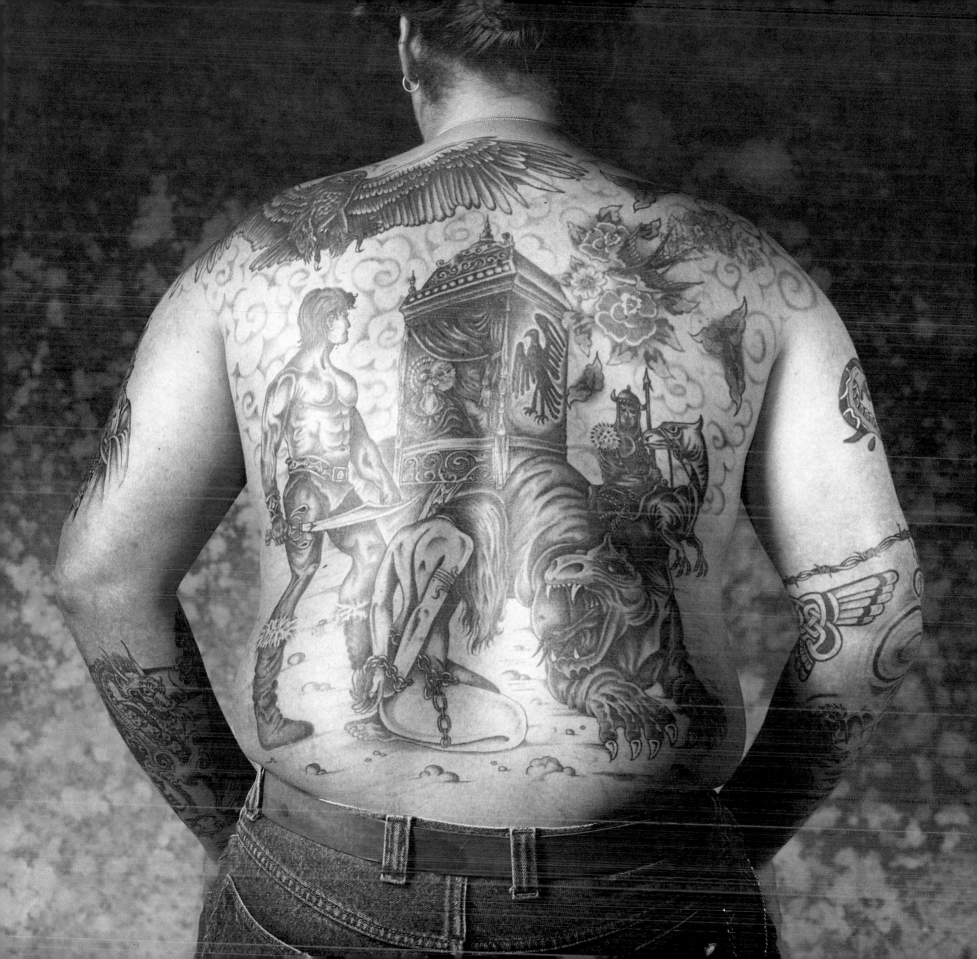

Left: Masculine strength, embodied by the eagle, a symbol of power which defies death, is further emphasised by the Maori moko proudly displayed on the chest. René is Dutch. It has taken him ten years to perfect these designs. He is a fan of horror films and says that he is also fascinated by the sorcery practised in the Middle Ages. This tattoo has a particularly macabre tone due to the cascade of skulls across the chest.

Right: Veiling the body in a seductive scarf, this cascade of flowers is undeniably erotic, as well as rich in symbolism. The flowers, butterflies and birds are feminine motifs. The sexual connotations of the humming bird, with his phallic beak, are particularly obvious. The flowers are Day Lilies, also known as Belle de Jour, because they bloom for such a short time. They symbolise the transitory nature of beauty.

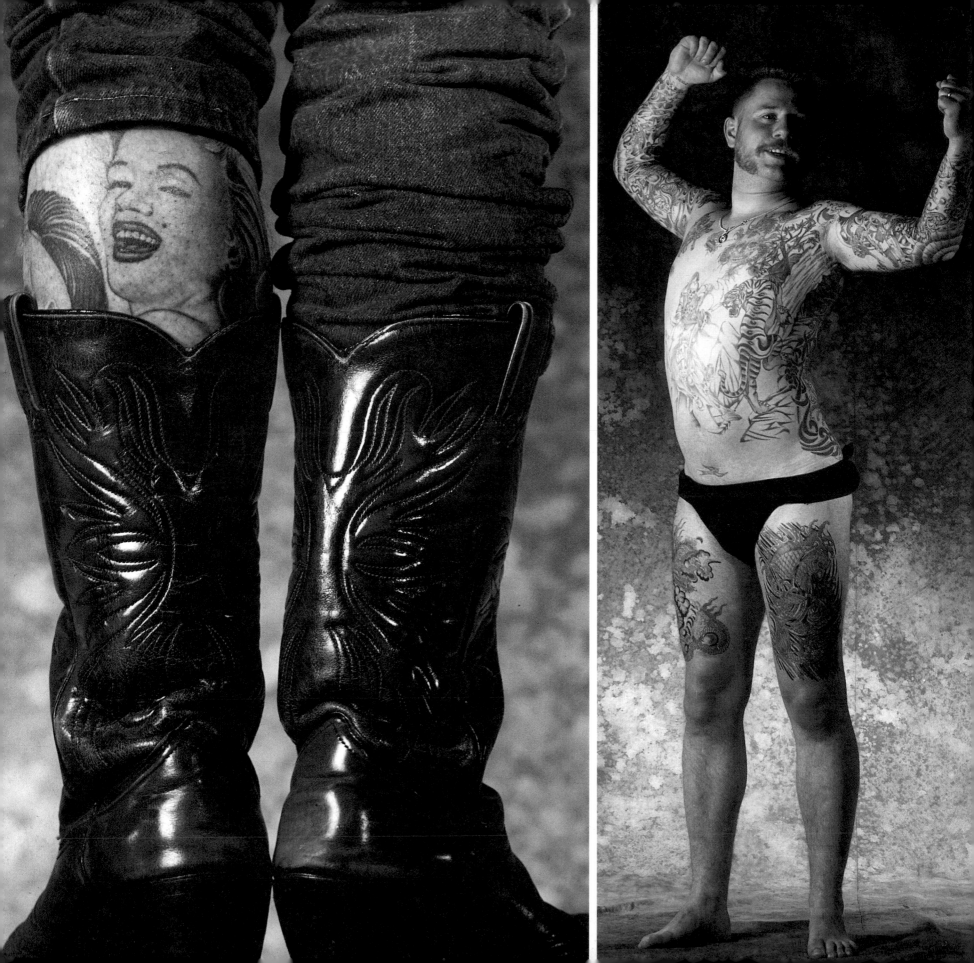

Left: Eternal Marilyn - he's got her under his skin!

Centre: Proudly showing off his array of fierce and mythical animals, this security guard swells his chest and takes centre stage. The images, which are slightly kitsch, are reminiscent of naive painting.

Right: The tattooist, as much sculptor as designer, plays games with the contours of the anatomy. A flower blooms from the navel, a dragon extends his claws across the pectorals, as if getting a better grip on the body. The human canvas of the skin brings to life the images which are outlined on it, allowing the wildest dreams and fantasies to emerge.

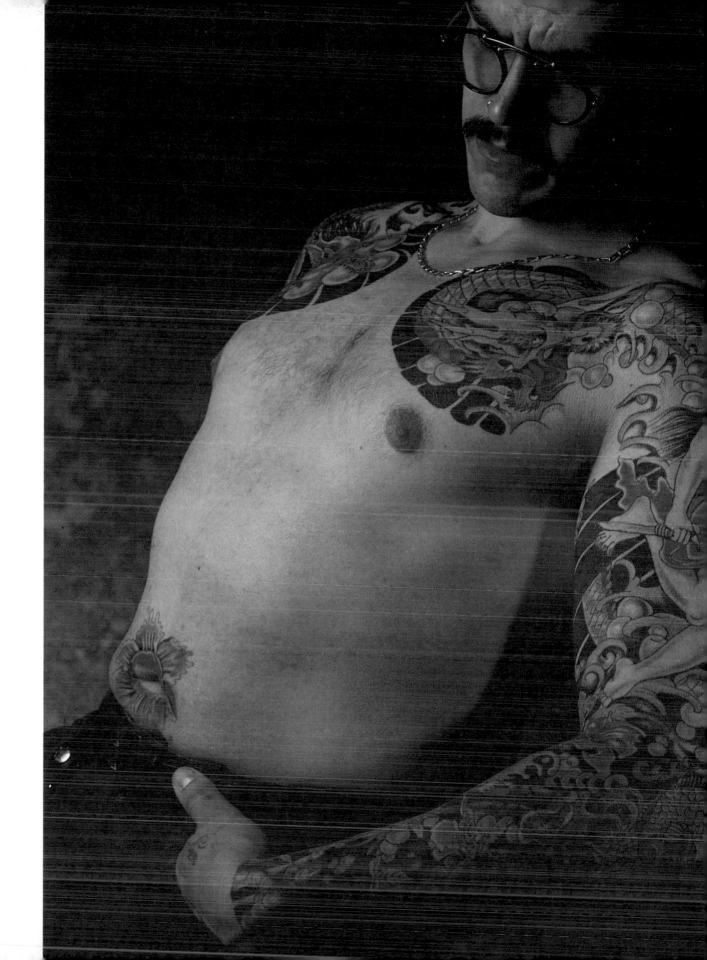

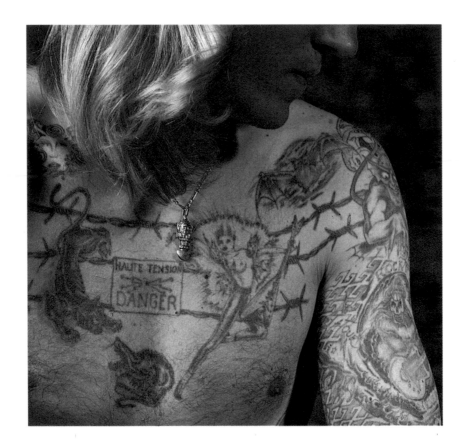

Left: "Danger! High voltage!" or "Touch at your peril".... Is this the real meaning of this pun which is stuck on the body? This tattoo collector has travelled the world to be tattooed by the most famous specialists.

Right: This is an overt fantasy of sexual submission, yet it is tattooed on a man who describes himself as very gentle. The eagle, a symbol of virility and power, is chained and held captive on a lead by an amazon woman.

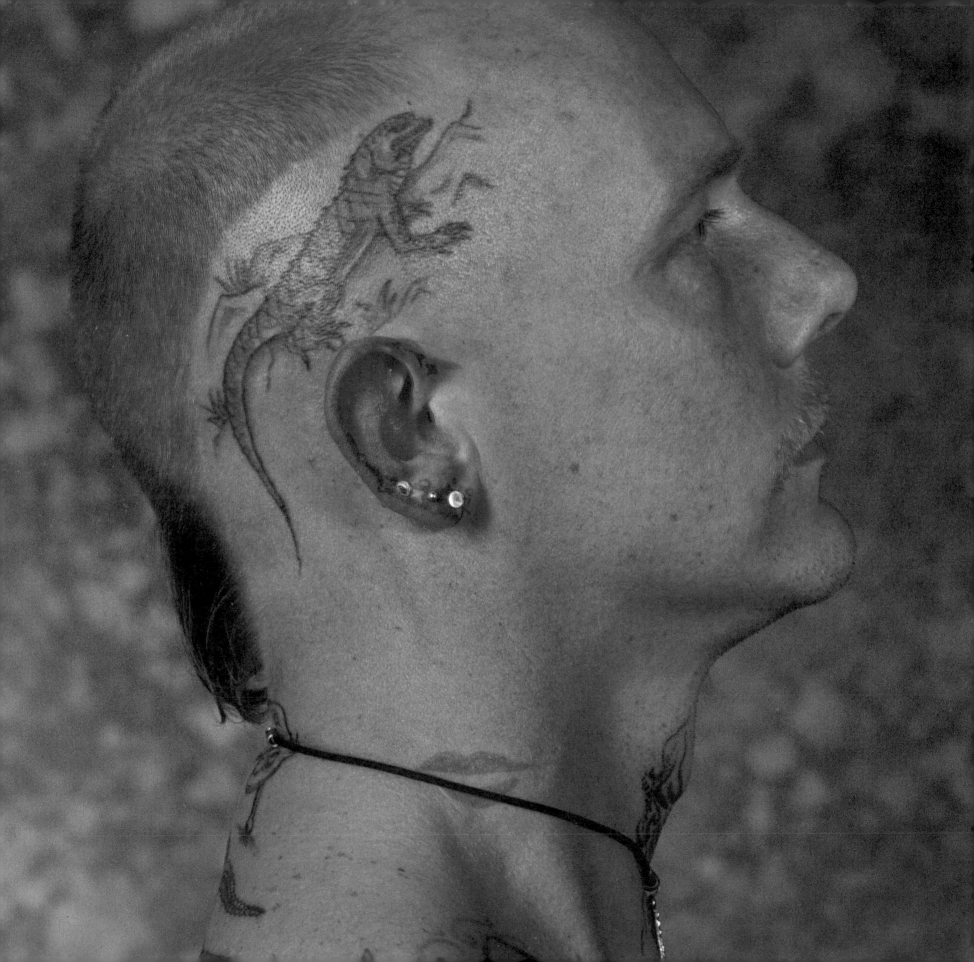

NARCISSISTIC TATTOOING

In primitive civilisations the tattoo is not only an indication of status, but also a form of decoration, particularly in those societies where minimal, if any clothing is worn. It clothes the skin and, since the origins of man, it has been linked with love of ornament and the cult of the body. Man is narcissistic, which isn't such a terrible fault. He not only likes to please himself, but also to appear desirable to others. He exists through the regard of others.

However poor or deprived he might be, homo sapiens takes pleasure in decorating his smooth body with trinkets. He is sensitive to the looks which he receives from others and likes to see himself reflected there. Gazing into the mirror, he would love to be able to make it tell him, if not that he is the most handsome, then at least that he is accepted, loved and acknowledged as unique. For then he feels that he exists........

In our society, which doesn't celebrate the ageing process, unlike other cultures, in which old people are revered, one is constantly under pressure to modify one's appearance, in order to remain youthful and desirable. It is necessary to adapt the appearance to an ideal, which varies according to culture and fashion.

Therefore the body is constantly recreated. It is tanned, shaved, deoderised, perfumed, made-up. It can be tattooed, modelled like clay by physical exercise, or sculpted by plastic surgery. Tanning, which suggests a life of leisure, gives it a healthy glow. Make-up disguises, smooths out imperfections and emphasises the strong points, such as an oval face, a sensual mouth or bright eyes.

The body, sculpted by beauty treatments, presents its canvas to the tattooist to become a graffiti, a tableau or an engraving.

Tattooing, more than any other form of adornment, fulfils a basic need in a way which the skin is unable to do. It fulfils the role of interface. It extends the inner space, thereby creating a distance from society, whilst enabling a dialogue to take place

Those with a passion for tattooing make use of every inch of the anatomy to accommodate their desired illustrations. The ear is embroidered, pierced, inlaid. A mouth has left a permanent kiss on the neck, a lizard has settled on the head to catch the sun. In Africa the lizard is a familiar sight around the house and is revered for its role as benevolent mediator with the gods. So perhaps It's In a strategic position here!

- a dialogue which is understood by the initiates.

Unwinding down the spine or encircling the arm, tattoos draw the eye along endless spirals and seem to amplify the body. The vivid colours of the tattoo leap out and attract the line of vision. The eye jumps from an azure blue to a blood red which is both hypnotic and disturbing.

The significance of different symbols can be determined from the colours, which reveal the most profound urges of the individual. In the Christian tradition, colours emanate from the light which translates the word of God. Therefore Christian artists, sensitive to these divine reflections, associate white with chastity, green with hope, blue with divine essence, black with penitence and red with lust. These colours are rooted in the subconscious and are chosen according to circumstances and the nature of the message to be conveyed.

Red is universally recognised as the colour of blood. In Africa it is the colour of life and fertility, whereas in China it represents death, and, in the west, desire and passion, culminating in annihilation.

Black, the colour of the night, symbolises ordeal, suffering, mourning, mystery. It is used as a charm against evil, which is the reason why black animals are sacrificed in witchcraft.

White, the colour of light, brilliance and purity is a good omen. Magic properties are often attributed to milk, especially woman's milk.

Green is a calming, positive colour, which symbolises growth, vegetation, spring and hope.

Yellow, the colour of gold and the sun, illuminates and energises.

The malleable body lends itself to metamorphosis. Convex chest, sculpted by exercise or emblazoned with an imperial eagle, biceps bulging from physical training or swelled by a haughty jaguar, thighs shaped by jogging or adorned with the image of a darting butterfly - every part of the anatomy carries an investment of some sort.

The Apollo of the gym feels as if he possesses superhuman strength. The man who has a roaring lion emerging from his shirt collar or a majestic eagle spreading its wings across his back is also displaying his power. The eagle, messenger of the sun and representative of Zeus, is the emblem of warriors and conquerors. From Caesar to the feudal knights to Napoleon it has accompanied the greatest heroes.

The jaguar, with eyes as sharp as its claws, exudes menace. Poised on the biceps, it appears to be waiting to pounce on its prey when the muscle is flexed. This proud and mysterious animal is the emblem of a wild and untameable character.

A simple flower can become a garland as its bearer becomes intent on perfecting the image.

A panther lies on a bed of peonies, serene and powerful. It gives birth to young which couple with horses, dragons and lizards to create a bestiary worthy of Noah's ark. The imagination runs wild, giving rise to cackling parrots, opulent orchids, clumps of hibiscus plundered by hummingbirds.........

The tattooed individual, like the body builder, often takes a narcissistic look at himself. The ornament becomes flesh and the flesh becomes ornament....a game of masquerade, tattooing personalises, protects or exhibits.

Racked with worry about what the future holds, human beings need to feel that they are beautiful and powerful. The ability to control the elements and one's own nature is achieved by artifice. Likewise seduction depends on appearance.

Just as the body builder shapes his body, restructures and refines it, the tattooed person transforms his body into images. He is seeking extravagance. The anatomy, colourfully packaged, attracts attention without fully exposing itself.

Concepts of beauty and ugliness vary according to different cultures. For example, the Haidas women with their extended lips holding plates inlaid with seashells horrified the French sailors who landed in Canada with La Pérouse, who subsequently recorded this encounter: "The women observe a custom which makes them appear quite hideous and which I

23 J-F La Pérouse: Voyage de La Pérouse, 1785-1788 - Paris, La Renaissance du livre, 1930, page 117

would have found hard to believe, had I not witnessed it myself. They all have their lips slit across the entire width of their mouth at the level of the gums, and carry a handleless wooden bowl pressed against the gums. The slit lip supports the bowl in such a way that the lower part of the mouth protrudes about two or three inches. We are trying to persuade them to give up this ornament. They are reluctant to do so, displaying the same embarrassed reaction as a European woman would if her breasts were uncovered." [23] A form of coquetry in one culture can appear as barbaric mutilation to another.

  The body, inscribed and glorified in primitive tribes, was ignored and even despised in the west, where the mind and spirit took precedence, until the beginning of this century. Christianity is mainly responsible for the dichotomy which was established between the body and the soul - to be preoccupied with the body indicated neglect of the soul. Nevertheless, the corporal envelope was liberated by various cultural movements in the sixties. The body regained its power of expression and, in particular, its erogenous value.

EROTIC TATTOOING

A true garment for the primitive man, the tattoo can replace clothes in those countries where clothing is considered to be inadequate or even useless as a status symbol. The tattoo not only provides everyone with a social identity, a unique persona, a touch of originality - but it also embellishes the body. It sends out erotic messages.

Tattoo is like make-up: it attracts attention, seduces or threatens the observer, warns him to keep his distance. It catches others in the trap of its appearance, whilst concealing true desires. It elevates ordinary beauty to a superior form of beauty. The observer is fascinated, hypnotised. The body becomes extraordinary and therefore more attractive.

In every culture, sexual attraction is determined by physical beauty, even if the definition of beauty differs from country to country. An African proverb states that beauty is not innate, but depends on the inscriptions made on the body. Only the scarified woman is attractive. The keloid - deliberately induced scar tissue - has an erogenous quality, especially in the pubic area.

In our society, the individual, a slave to appearance, is constantly looking at himself. He checks that his image conforms to what he wants, and readjusts it if its reflection in the mirror or the observer's eyes is unacceptable to him. Human beings are always recreating themselves to make themselves attractive and to feel that they exist through their impact on others. For some, tattooing is a means to achieve this narcissistic rejuvenation and stand out from the crowd, especially for those who feel that they have been cheated by nature but don't want to participate in the conventional fashion games of our society.

In Egypt the thighs of dancers were tattooed with the image of Bes, god of licentious pleasures. As soon as the dance began these images were set in motion and captivated the audience.

In the Marquesas Islands the women inscribe their

fingers with spirals, which twist and turn as they carry out their daily tasks. Housework is thereby discreetly eroticised and becomes a magic process. For the men, beautiful tattoos are an emblem of pride. The hunters and warriors adorn their thighs and shoulders with stylised animals and curves which interact with the contours of the muscles. These subtle arabesques attract the eye and draw it along the musculature, as if pressing the observer to acknowledge the strength and power of the man. The status of the bearer determines the richness of the designs and colouring, and, therefore his charm. So chiefs have certain privileges.............

Tattoos are an essential element of the seduction process for the Aborigine male and are usually an essential preliminary to marriage. In New Zealand tattooists are on a level with sculptors and painters, modelling the body in accordance with one rule of perfection: harmony.

The Maori women of New Zealand and the Ainus women of Hokkeido Island in Japan would emphasise their lips with blue whorls to fulfil their ideal of beauty. The Maya women of the pre-Colombian era had already adopted this artifice, using tar. In our sophisticated western civilisation it is sometimes difficult to understand these seduction criteria. However the same motivation exists in western women who have their lips outlined by "aesthetic tattooing" or swelled by collagen injections. Full lips are, without a doubt, more erotic.

Naked skin provokes. Tattooed skin is suggestive because it conceals and exposes simultaneously. An undergarment, the tattoo allows one to hide behind a network of intertwinings, creating a type of second skin. It is always there as the ultimate protection against the gaze of the voyeur, even during a provocative striptease. It can also add spice to a relationship. It is a sort of intermediate state between the naked skin and clothes. It protects, reassures and decorates, but it also veils and maintains the mystery. It provides an outline while diverting the eye from the essence.

The tattooed woman is like the fairytale mermaid, a sort of hybrid creature, which represents both the civilised and the animal state. The height of ambiguity. Like the mermaid or siren, the tattooed woman represents feminine duplicity in the juxtaposition of appearance and reality, the visible and the concealed. The contradictions give her a mysterious quality which is both frightening and fascinating. She distances herself from nature, but simultaneously affirms her role within nature. The mermaid, an ultra-feminine symbol, with her beautiful voice and long, flowing hair, is intriguing because of her asexual tail, covered in cold, slimy scales - a sign of her deception. She bewitches sailors with her songs and hypnotises them with her strange beauty in order to drag them down to the ocean depths for a cannibal feast.

The colourful mantle of the tattooed woman is disconcerting. She tends to choose butterflies, small birds and flowers to affirm her femininity. These light-hearted motifs are playful and arousing. They are reminiscent of the beauty spots worn by "loose women" in the 18th century, which, by means of their location on the face, sent a clear message of invitation to any potential Casanova. Tattoos are carefully positioned to direct attention and desire towards a certain part of the body, usually the most voluptuous parts, such as breasts and buttocks. The western woman is adopting methods similar to those of the African woman, who draws attention to her legs by wearing pearl ankle bracelets and adorns herself with elaborate scarifications.

These adornments are irresistably attractive, but the woman who is covered with tattoos is a match for the toughest man. She distances her body to turn it into an exhibit, thereby taking on an almost mythical appearance. Star, goddess or super-human, she becomes untouchable. She represents a sacred body in comparison with the mundane and profane. Protected by her decorations like the mermaid, she takes pleasure in uttering a challenge to men.

Tattooing creates areas of light and shade on the body. It unveils certain regions of flesh, whilst hiding the essential. It is this semi-nakedness which arouses the senses because it retains an element of mystery and allows dreams of discovery........... Tattooing is to nudity what a gourmet meal is to a gourmand: someone who appreciates the colour and harmony of the dishes and who recognises that the appearance and presentation hold a promise of what is inside: someone who inhales and remembers, just as Proust immortalised his grandmother's madeleines: someone who swirls the wine around his mouth to savour its body and smoothness ......He analyses, captures the moment to defer and anticipate the pleasure. The art is to make the mouth water, to distil the sensuality, like a striptease.

The Japanese have become the masters of this art. The erotic quality of their tattoos is widely acknowledged as part of the charm of the Far East. The Japanese civilisation, unlike our Greco-Latin based culture, disregards anatomy for its own sake, and attaches much more value to the quality of the accessories.

The Japanese woman, even the prostitute, is never completely naked. Always perfectly coiffed and made-up, she offers herself in a wave of fabric. The draped cloth, a subtle sheath, veils and unveils, tricks and conceals. It is a highly refined game. "The envelope itself is consecrated like a precious, though gratuitous object: the packaging is a thought..........The layered perfection of this envelope postpones the discovery of its contents, which are often insignificant.......Its value lies in what it hides, protects and in the signals it sends out...........Often the revelation of its contents is postponed until much later ....The envelope is the focus, and the object itself becomes unreal - a mirage....." [24] The Japanese woman, like a carefully wrapped sweet, allows herself to be uncovered slowly and admired. As Barthes says, pleasure lies in gradual discovery, rather than in consummation.

The tattoo is an additional layer, another envelope

24 Roland Barthes: L'empire des signes - Skira, Les sentiers de la création collection, Champs Flammarion, 1970.

which prolongs delight. A mischevious bird of paradise dips into a large peony blooming on a white shoulder. Dragons and snakes lasciviously coil themselves from the neck to the pubis. A butterfly is poised on a hip - an invitation to pleasure. There is a hint of nudity behind the adornment.

Coloured skin draws the eye and ensnares it. Once captured, the gaze lingers on the colour and texture of the skin and follows the journey of the humming bird and serpent. It travels from wrist to elbow, up the length of the arm, caresses the neck, slides into the hollow of the shoulder, descends to the armpit, hesitates, then moves softly down the breast towards the nipple. Then it moves downwards again, pauses on the belly to study its contours, and wanders along the length of the thigh, until it disappears and is lost for good in the dark, secret space below............

There was one particular type of tattoo which aroused a great deal of attention in the past. Jokingly called irozemi, from "iro," which not only means colour - although this tattoo is always monochrome - but also sexual pleasure, this tattoo was only visible when the blood rushed to the surface of the skin. Practically invisible under normal circumstances, it appeared in negative when provoked by a state of drunkenness or pleasure or simply by a hot bath. It was only found on women and was reputed to be very painful and extremely dangerous, since it was achieved by using white lead, which was a known health hazard. The burning of desire and the pain of open wounds were combined to arouse the senses and flirt with death. The same erotic connotations emerge in Tanizaki's novel Shisei (The Tattooist), written in 1910, which provided the inspiration for the film La Femme Tatouée. The definition of tattooing is expressed as pain in pleasure, pleasure in tearing the flesh, aesthetic suffering. This form of tattoo is always done manually with a single needle to provoke a sharper, more acute pain.

The tattooing and piercing of the individual's most intimate areas represents the ultimate boundary of sexual perversion. Piercing is almost always an evolution, or an extension of the practice of tattooing. "It is very rare that an individual goes in for body piercing without having been tattooed first" declares Bruno, a tattooist in Pigalle, Paris. This really is a case of going full circle, since it brings us back to the Pacific region. In Borneo, infibulation is also part of the initiation rites.

An erotic tattoo, even if it is roughly depicted, is never vulgar or openly pornographic, with the exception of certain sexual "graffiti" such as a crudely represented phallus or finger......Tattooing is a sensual form of expression, like wearing silk, leather or fur on bare skin, like a soft caress. It is not an end in itself, but a means to arouse the libido. With its outrageous colours the tattoo evokes the gaudy make-up, lace and trinkets of the prostitute. These accessories are indispensible for the realisation of certain fantasies - they eroticise the woman's body and spark off fetishist yearnings.

The tattooed body exhibits itself as if issuing a challenge, veiling itself in artifice to arouse desire. Those who are tattooed transfigure themselves by means of a skilful trompe l'oeil, trying to thwart death, which is, unfortunately, the only certainty that exists.

These manipulations of the body are an attempt to evade the trap of time. Because youth is synonymous with seduction in every culture, the body is cut here, scarred there, remodelled elsewhere, pumped up or lifted, and generally tortured to remain young and beautiful, fulfilling the saying "One must suffer in order to be beautiful." Men sculpt their biceps and pectorals to try to emulate the athletes of ancient Greece, while women try to trim fleshy thighs or lift drooping breasts. Chinese women subject themselves to terrible pain to keep their feet tiny and thereby remain attractive according to their traditional ideal of beauty. African women retouch and augment their scarifications to arouse the desire of their men .... All these modifications are an effort of will, as strong as it is

useless, to oppose the irrevocable - the great equaliser. However, paradoxically, they also presage death itself, the ultimate metamorphosis of the body.

Whether or not is it acknowledged, the goal of many of these strategically placed and therefore erotic tattoos is surely to seduce the observer into sexual submission by means of fascination - fascination with the mark itself and with the abnormality it represents. A new code is established between the eye and the skin, based on illusion, dream, desire and a disconcerting strangeness. Through this game of fascination, the observer is drawn out of himself, and, in a way, invaded and possessed by the person whom he is observing.

Sexual exhibitionism has found an alibi of decency in tattooing. For women, who are naturally more exhibitionist than men according to tattooists, the areas of preference for tattoos are the breasts, hips, the pubis, and, above all, the thighs. A tattoo at the top of the thigh is supposed to be irresistible. This is nothing new, as the Micronesian women have always tattooed themselves on the thigh to arouse their partners and stimulate fertility. Prostitutes in particular tattoo themselves there in the hope of attracting clients more easily.

The tattoo bestows a special sort of prestige. The tattooed man represents the virile male figure, a macho type, who attracts both women and homosexuals. Could it be that enthusiasts of this type of image are really fetishists, who are reluctant to admit it?

Colourful skin is a narcissistic way of declaring the worth and power of the individual. At the meetings where initiates gather together, they undress and take pleasure in displaying themselves to the curious, approving eyes of the novices and converts.

The skin is one of the main components of adult sexuality. Does it have an auto-erotic quality for the tattooed individual, who marks himself like a masochist inflicting pain to gain pleasure? There seems to be a certain pleasure in committing a raid on the body; the act of puncturing becomes an act of penetration, the pain of which is eroticised. This pain gives rise to the belief that the relationship between tattooist and tattooed is uneasy and confused, and possibly akin to a sort of sadomasochistic rapport. The skin becomes a receptacle for a coloured substance injected by the tattooist's needle in a state of pain and ecstasy.

ARTISTIC TATTOOING

"Give him bright colours to paint his body, so that he shines a beautiful red in the land of souls."
SCHILLER

In tattooing, the whole body becomes an ornamental surface and the basis for an artistic expression which everyone interprets in their own way. Often dismissed as banal graffiti, or street art, tattooing is aligned with the popular traditional art of the nomadic tribes, which can resemble naive art or, sometimes, a pictorial masterpiece. Some tattooed people have photo albums of their own tattoos, like a collection of paintings. The classic old masters have been succeeded by voluptuous slashes, bright splashes of colour which pierce and blister. Lacking artistic talent of their own, the tattooed individuals offer their bodies as canvas. Some travel around the world searching for the prize which is worthy of the beauty and delicacy of the work engraved on their flesh. They look at themselves and admire themselves in a totally self-sufficient relationship. They exhibit themselves as if they were on show in a gallery, and expose themselves to enthusiasts, who, surprised at first, gradually become captivated by this display. The wandering eye is drawn to these unfamiliar and surprising marks, trying to decipher the message which they might convey. No-one remains indifferent to the curious art of tattooing.

Graffiti for the soul

"Many tattoo designs are derived from slang. To liven up the image, endow the underlying thoughts with more profundity and to make the expression more vivid, the criminal shapes his tattoos in the style of an allegory; sometimes of Latin origin, but usually from ancient Greek, in which almost every concept and element was personified. Death became a skeleton armed with a scythe; time, an old man carrying an hourglass; justice, a blindfolded woman holding scales in her hand." [25]

   Many people believe that inscriptions on the skin are merely an attempt at artistic expression, similar to the painting of a child, who can barely write. Defiant annotations, hasty, slapdash designs scrib-

25 William Caruchet: Bas-fonds du crime et tatouages - Editions du Rocher, 1981

bled with a needle - in a bar or a cell - they undoubtedly bear some relation to the graffiti which abounds on the walls of our cities. They also reflect a childish sort of insolence.

Like graffiti, tattooing is an incision, a scratch - in the etymological sense of the word - an engraving on a surface which is soft enough to be penetrated. It stems from the same anxieties and the same needs. It is a spontaneous expression of a feeling of urgency, of the physiological urge to survive, and its symbolic lexicon is not always easy to decipher.

Graffiti and tattooing tend to find expression in the same sort of places, usually where slang is the common language - on the streets, in prisons, in barracks, in so-called working class environments. Many vengeful coded signs developed in the prisons: such as three dots at the base of the thumb, meaning "Death to the pigs"; one dot on each finger joint, "Screw justice"; four aces, " I stab you through the heart, steal your money and leave you lying on the ground"; the dagger of vengeance, the cross or the criminals' patron saint........ These signs, which are incomprehensible to the uninitiated, are used as signals between initiates. Like slang, it is a crude and basic language, which indicates that the people using it all belong to a certain group.

In this form of expression, only the structure varies. Skin replaces stone, but the gestures and themes are identical. Both painting walls and painting bodies have connotations of defilement and profanation, and the thrill of the forbidden, especially if the message is provocative.

These irreverent signs and symbols are the preferred mode of expression of any protest, poised in between familiar writing and clumsy, childish drawing. These naive graphics, either disapproved of or merely tolerated by the majority, are addressed to the world at large. They are deliberately and defiantly displayed on the visible parts of the body, just as they are on the walls. The clumsiness and the stylised distortion of the lines evoke the grotesque and monstrous figures which are so popular with children. Aggression or licentiousness appears to be the message in much of this communication: violence, death and sex are favourite topics.

The motif of the heart, so widespread in western iconography, represents romantic love, but there is a tendency to forget that it is also an erotic symbol. The pierced heart can be an image of carnal love. As well as the heart, other more abstract signs, such as leaf-like forms, triangles, diamonds and targets, have feminine connotations, whilst arrows are often a representation of the phallus. A stake has connotations of penetration. These stereotypes have retained their meaning in Indo-European erotic iconography since the prehistoric age.

The charm of this vocabulary lies in its ambivalence, its equivocal nature - fascinating because it is sombre, unfamiliar, disconcerting, chilling..........

The sort of black romanticism which emanates from some of the slightly macabre or perverse designs hints at the beauty contained in pain and deprivation. A strange beauty which lies outside of normal conventions and customs, and which, to quote Shelley, is endowed with "the grace of horror."

But this type of image can represent a deliverance from, and thus a sort of victory over anguish: the anguish of death conjured up by a fantastic array of satanic creatures - rats, vultures, scorpions - and skull and crossbones; the anguish of being alone, incarcerated within four walls, as signified by the number five on a die tattooed on the back of a convict's hand. The image robs the spell of its power by dissipating the menace it contains.

One major discovery which revealed certain parallels between tattoos and graffiti was that of the cave paintings of early man - the forerunners of our mural inscriptions - and of his statuettes marked with red ochre - the first indications of the practice of tattooing. It is probable that these first stone age traces of human life are the results of Neanderthal man's need to communicate. Paintings or engravings, they are undeniably works of art. The spontaneous sketches - galloping reindeer, bison, wild horses on the run - given eternal life in these dark caverns by lines, dots, shades of ochre and black - are a surprising sort of impressionism. These works suggest that, by this stage, man had established his superiority over the rest of nature to such a degree that he not only had some leisure time but also the urge to express himself creatively in artistic form. However, his urge to do this probably arose in part from the belief that, by representing the wild animals which surrounded him, he could, in some way, protect himself from the dangers which they presented. It may also have played a role in some of his rituals, in which the animal was worshipped as a god or totem.

More than forty thousand years later, the graffiti artist and the tattooed individual have rediscovered the essential elements of languages which date from time immemorial. One can still see graffiti on the ruins of Pompeii or on the Maya temples. Ancient texts and engravings also record the long history of tattooing. The lover who scribbles the name of his girlfriend inside a heart pierced with an arrow, or the schoolboy who caricatures his teacher on the desk have not invented anything new. Neither has the man who marks himself forever with a panther stabbed through the heart by a dagger. Throughout the ages the child which exists inside every man and woman has introduced an element of playfulness and poeticism into life. The tiniest scribble is a form of art.

A popular art form for thousands of years

There are many similarities between tattooing and the popular art of the nomadic tribes.

Along with dancing and singing, visual art was a part of the folklore and traditions of these primitive tribes, particularly in the Pacific islands and among the Berber and Indian tribes.

The same symbols and calligraphic motifs are found on the skin, in architecture, on clothes, car-

pets and domestic objects. Three thousand years ago they were found on Mycenean pottery and neolithic amulets.

None of the representations is truly figurative. Flowers, plants and animals are reproduced in a stylised manner, and, in the most primitive designs, merely consist of dots, lines and curves. The format of these designs follows a specific set of traditional rules, which have been passed down, verbally, from generation to generation.

The designs of the Maghreb take the form of the famous "silaya" - a stylised palm tree - outlined on the forehead, or the alfalfa leaf - a lucky charm dating back to the pre-Islamic era and a symbol of Allah's protection.

The choice of motifs, like that of the colours, is made according to certain archetypes. These are no doubt rooted in a sort of collective unconscious, of the type cited by Jung, and common to all civilisations. Ethnologists have always been struck by the recurrence of certain formal structures. They can be found on the weapons and domestic objects of the Pacific region, in the paintings on the huts of the American Indians and in the decoration of archaic Chinese vases. The fact that these symbols are identical suggests that primitive beliefs were also identical in some respects.

For example, the spiral is found in all civilisations, regardless of the epoch. It is universally recognised as the link which unites all races and peoples together in the quest for immortality. Over the course of centuries this figure has evolved into more complicated representations, such as a herringbone pattern, entwined knots, a hooked wheel or cross - swastika - culminating in the perfect circle, often depicted by the "ourobouros" or serpent biting its own tail. All these decorative motifs - common in the Mediterranean region, the oriental countries of the Byzantine Empire, India, China, America and Africa - fulfil a magic or religious role, as well as aesthetic. They are fundamental elements of the Taoist yin and yang symbolism. [26] They are linked to life and death and to man's existential quest.

It is no coincidence that, on abandoning his cave, prehistoric man constructed circular huts from branches, following the example of animals, insects and birds. Nor is it a coincidence that the dwellings of the Eskimos, Indians and Pygmies - igloos, tepees and huts - all have a circular base. The circle, which is considered to be the fundamental basis of architecture and the original artistic expression of man, also fulfils a magic function. It represents the cocoon, the nest, the shell which man and animals inhabit before birth, and which they are always trying to recreate. The circle, an endless line, represents both a finite shape and a state of perpetual motion, providing a lasting and ubiquitous symbol of continuous renewal, resurrection and eternity. It is also interesting to observe that the reflex action of a child who is given a pencil, but doesn't know how to write, is to scribble circles, or at least curved shapes. Is this possibly a sign of a hereditary impulse?

The basic spiral form is found in the designs of most civilisations, but the Celts were the first to use double, triple and quadruple spirals, which required a high level of mathematical and geometric accuracy and were therefore very sophisticated art forms. Although the Maoris were widely acknowledged as the masters of the art of curved lines, Celtic art appears to be much more intricate.

In Maori art, the curves of the lines in the famous mokos resemble waves breaking on the shore or the tree ferns of New Zealand. An emblem of power and an object of pride, the moko bestows immortality on the chief of the tribe, as his head is preserved by his descendants. It is ironic that this tradition died out as a result of colonisation and the ensuing greed of morbid collectors. There were too many incidences of crimes committed on behalf of these ardent "collectors" in 19th century England in order to acquire a good head! The contemporary Maoris still make up their faces like their ancestors for traditional festivals. Is this merely a gesture for

26 From one of the oldest philosophies, the Tao symbol is formed by two spirals going in opposite directions, which represent opposing energy forces.

the tourists, or, as in the past, is it an attempt to communicate with the gods?

The manuscripts of the Irish Celts were illustrated with knots, plaits and winding braids and chains in figure-of-eight patterns. This form of art, which first emerged over five centuries ago, now only exists as vague traces on blocks of stone in the Shetland Islands, Scotland, Scandinavia and what was formerly known as Gaul. It has really only retained its popularity in Irish traditional art. Within the context of our more classical art, this type of knotwork and plaiting reached the height of its popularity during the Gothic period, when it was a prominent feature of the stained glass rose windows. With their labyrinths of medallions, symbols and legends, these windows offer a view of an enchanting universe. They resemble cobwebs which shimmer with the light of their captive jewels and the reflection of rays from another sun - more generous than our own ....Was it some sort of mystical goal which motivated Leonardo da Vinci, Albrecht Dürer and Michelangelo to make such abundant use of the curved form in their works?

When he engraves decorative arabesques on his skin, is the tattooed individual merely intent on transforming his flesh into a jewel or a piece of lace. Or is he reweaving the threads which unite him with his ancestors? Only he can answer that question.

These links with the past and ancient traditions are clear in tribal tattooing. But the current resurgence of minimalist graphics indicates that many of those who are tattooed are moving away from the more figurative images. Sometimes the tattooists who specialise in tribal tattooing are criticised for adopting the easiest approach. But the advocates of this trend, known as "new tribalism" or "modern primitive", particularly well known specialists, such as Léo Zulueta, Dan Thomé and Frank Boas, have pointed out that they are merely reflecting the evolution of modern painting. In a similar way to abstract art, a refined, purer style has replaced figurative images, which are now considered to be too simplistic as a means of expression. However the tattooist must take into account other potential complications. The background to the tattoo is neither white nor flat, and, furthermore, it is mobile. The tattooist has to make allowances for anatomy, and, in addition to being a graphic artist, he must also become a "spatialist" - with the ability to manipulate and exploit the distortions of his canvas caused by the movements of the body.

The body then becomes an image, as the tattooist does not merely apply illustrations onto the skin, like a transfer. He conveys a message of harmony by means of the form of his designs and their location on strategic areas of the body.

What makes tribal tattooing interesting, according to its devotees, is that it never becomes outdated. From the Dayaks of Borneo to contemporary tattooists, the choice of motifs correspond to universal archetypes, which are recognised and understood throughout the world. Stylised animal symbols - lizards, scorpions, birds, dogs - are accompanied by mystical inscriptions. Even the most inventive variations on the basic form adhere to the rules governing the unity and the associations of the basic motifs, which follow a very specific code. Tattooing retains its mystery because it is part of a world which is far removed from the banal, everyday domain of man.

Tattooing iconography embraces an extraordinary array of symbols linked with immortality. Whether it is circles, Celtic knots, serpents, dragons or other stylised mythical creatures, such as the phoenix of the oriental countries, it always seems as if the tattooed person wants to invoke death. The tattoo is a language which is cemented onto the skin and represents something much more significant than a piece of jewellery which can be removed or changed.

Tattooing, a naive art

Although tribal tattooing represents a quest for purity, the common motifs are usually copied and merely traced by the tattooist. Often the person who is going to be tattooed, lacking in imagination, just leafs through a catalogue and selects a stereotyped panther or rose. This is far removed from true artistic creation. It is merely a transfer.

Sometimes the tattooist considers himself to be a naturalist or naive painter. He enters into the fairytale world or animal kingdom to escape from uniformity.

He displays his ferocious or mythical animals with pride, sticking out his chest and flexing his muscles, as if he were on show in a circus. He is compared to dwarves, giants, Siamese twins and all those bizarre, abnormal creatures who attract the curiosity of the onlookers who have come to view the spectacle. He could easily be a character in a Fellini or Greenaway film.

He transforms himself into a peasant painter, joining the ranks of Douanier Rousseau, the Haitian painters or those from the Yugoslavian Hlebine school. The designs are assembled side by side, randomly, without any thematic order, just following the imagination like a stream of consciousness.

Transcending the boundaries of tradition, tattooing, like naive painting, defies conventions. Both creative forms are located on the fringe of the art world and are not subject to its trends, their origins rooted in the depths of history and the cultural conscience. They inject freshness and spontaneity into our organised, standardised world, which is so lacking in poetry.

The tattoo can sometimes border on kitsch. The images, taken out of their normal context, are hyped so extravagantly that they are almost pathetic. Motifs and colours become more and more outrageous. But this incongruous series of reproductions on the skin - mermaids, dragons and daggers intertwined against a background of butterflies or exotic birds- can be the stimulus for either an extravagant creation, or, simply, a joke.

A Japanese engraving

Japanese tattooing is, without a doubt, the most spectacular and beautiful of all ornamental tattooing. It ranks as a masterpiece. The body clothes itself permanently in bracelets or doublets; in a coloured jacket, nonchalantly slung over the shoulder. It transforms itself into a living picture and becomes a fresco, a jewel, a poem.

The varied Japanese iconography is full of references - not only to the amazing adventures of the hero of *Suikoden*, but also to the folk tales and legends about bold Samurai warriors and wicked princesses. The tengou, a sort of gnome which haunts the mountains and forests, and plays tricks on humans, also features frequently in the designs from the land of the rising sun. He reminds man of his faults and teaches him humility. This type of figure is represented by the jester in our culture and by the goblin and the elf in the Scandinavian culture.

Generally speaking, the basic themes are taken from the mythology of the Far East, usually from a mixture of Japanese and Chinese legends. The animals of the zodiac, and especially those admired for their virility, such as the tiger, rooster or horse, rub shoulders with the phoenix - a mythical bird with the ability to resurrect itself from the ashes - and with the lightest of all, the butterfly. They embroider vivid shirts and scarves on the flesh; clothing with mysterious powers. Reputed to be a source of vigour and courage, Japanese tattooing can be used to intimidate an enemy, displaying threatening animals peering menacingly from biceps and pectorals. But a less menacing array of animals, gliding from the back of the neck to the thighs, can be just as effective as a means of seduction. The carp, a lucky omen and a creature much admired in Japan for its perseverance, is always much in demand, and swims around on the most beautiful backs.

However the dragon and the snake, incarnations of the entire spectrum of cosmic forces, are definitely the principal motifs, and those which are reproduced the most frequently. Masters of the earth and the sea, they represent the original, mystical body and the primordial form of the gods.

The red dragon, steed of the immortals, represents divine power and all things spiritual. From its kingdom high up in the heavens it spits down bolts of lightning, the fertilising fire. It represents yang, the masculine, source of life and strength.

The green dragon reigns over the seas, spitting out the primordial waters and jealously guarding the pearl in the depths of the sea. It represents yin, the feminine, hiding the secrets of conception in its belly. The search for the pearl represents the difficult search for the sublime essence which is concealed in the self - the quest for the Holy Grail. The acquisition of the pearl is the victory of the spirit over matter, the discovery of the core of everything and the attainment of wisdom. A symbol of the Emperor of China, a wise man amongst wise men, the dragon is often associated with the chrysanthemum, the emblem of the Japanese imperial family. It is synonymous with power and eternity.

The imagery of the Far East often depicts the two dragons locked in conflict - figures which are also often found in medieval art and in the caduceus. This represents the confrontation of opposing but complementary forces - shadows and light, low and high, feminine and masculine, yin and yang - the fight between reason and instinct.

The snake is an elusive entity. Endowed with the power of metamorphosis, it is associated with the world of the supernatural and sorcery. In the Sino-Japanese culture it has always represented the power and the knowledge of the Shaman. But it also excels as a harbinger of death. Capable of being both visible and invisible, it can effect transformation and transcendence. The analogy with Judeo-Christian beliefs is obvious. The snake in the Garden of Eden seduces Eve and instils in her the desire to identify with God by eating the forbidden fruit. For Adam and Eve taking a bite of the apple meant the acquisition of knowledge - knowledge of the differences between them, of God, of desire and envy. It signified the passage from a natural state to a state of knowledge.

The snake also has connotations of the concept of regeneration, which implies the ability to regress from the adult to the embryonic state. The association of the reptile with the umbilical cord, or, indeed, any other link, is still very common in contemporary Japanese rituals. Even though it is all-powerful, the snake is a conceptualisation of the indefinable, reduced to the nudity of a single line and is, therefore, constantly searching for its true identity. A perfect phallic symbol, it stiffens to represent the libido rising - the renewed manifestation of life. Represented by a perfect circle - the ourobouros - it is a symbol for nature recreating itself through self-consumption. Everything is a perpetual beginning. Inescapable death is, paradoxically, a condition of life.

In Japan the myths of Yamatotobime and Omononushi present sexuality as an incestuous cycle going back to the beginning of time. Killed by her husband, Yamatotobime is reincarnated in her son, Mikogami, symbolised by a snake. The murder of the woman, who represents all that is wild and natural, not only instils cultural order, but also makes it possible to rediscover the divine and invincible elements of nature.

The greatest supernatural power of man lies in his ability to distance himself from culture, to regress to an embryonic state and to metamorphise himself into the cosmic essence. This is a backward step, but one which is taken deliberately. This is the power symbolised by the snake, and which those who tattoo themselves are seeking.

Not all tattooed individuals are fully aware of the philosophy and symbolism associated with these tattoos derived from engravings. Often they are merely concerned with the aesthetic quality of the designs and are attracted to them because of the rich colours and the abundance of motifs.

Tattoos resemble an embroidered kimono of incomparable beauty. The background is often made up of the flowers of orchids and peach trees, which diminish the aggression displayed by many of the mythical animals. Symbols of spring and youth, these flowers represent passive, feminine characteristics. The head of the flower is a receptacle, like a cup or the female sex. It is fertilised in order to give birth and bear fruit. The flower is also a symbol of transitory beauty: the Day Lily or Belle de Jour, as its name indicates, is exceptionally beautiful, but only blooms for a very short time. Cherry blossoms, as ephemeral as the life of the Samurai, are used as a metaphor for the chivalrous spirit and sense of sacrifice of the Samurai. They represent the essential qualities of Japanese tradition.

It is surprising to note how many of the large repertoire of symbols relate to the notion of fertility, longevity and immortality. Maybe tattooing really is a form of protection against the ravages of time?

GUIDE TO TATTOOING

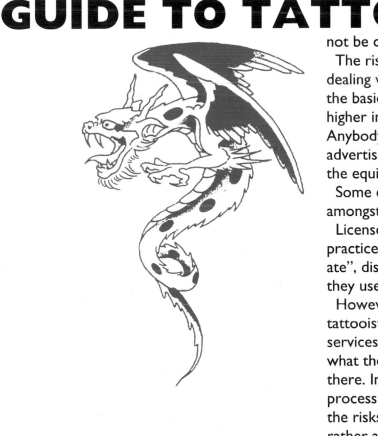

What are the risks involved in tattooing?

The tattoo is a puncture, a tear in the skin. So a secondary infection or the transmission of viral diseases is always a possibility. The threat of AIDS should be taken very seriously and the risk of hepatitis B should also not be underestimated. However, even so, tattooing should not be condemned out of hand.

The risk is minimal, virtually non-existent if one is dealing with a professional tattooist who observes the basic rules of hygiene. However the risk is much higher in the case of amateur, makeshift tattooists. Anybody can obtain a tattooing "kit" by placing advertisements in specialist magazines. In prisons the equipment is even more basic.

Some cases of HIV infection have been reported amongst prisoners who tattoo each other. [27]

Licensed tattooists adhere to a standard code of practice. They use surgical gloves when they "operate", disinfect their tools and sterilise them, and they use new needles for every customer.

However, currently no official sanitary controls of tattooists' premises are undertaken by the hygiene services. The customer, therefore, has to rely on what the tattooist tells him and on what he sees there. In theory, as the customer is undergoing this process of his own free will, he is responsible for the risks he runs by being tattooed. This is still rather a grey area in legal terms.

Although tattooists do not have a well defined status as yet, they are counted as independent workers. Affiliated with "literary and artistic illustrators", they pay a licence fee and taxes.

There is no diploma to prove their skill, but tattooists demand to be acknowledged as artists and want their profession to be officially recognised. They are strongly opposed to amateur tattooists, nicknamed "scratchers," as the clandestine practice of tattooing contributes to the bad press which they frequently receive. There are often conflicts

The code of ethics of the French Tattooing Association advises against tattooing any visible parts of the body, and particularly the face, since this type of adornment may lead to problems in the bearer's social life. In England and Holland the tattoo is an object of curiosity rather than criticism. This musician, tattooed by Hanky Panky in Amsterdam, gives the impression that he feels at ease in any context with his facial tattoo.

27 The Lancet, 1973
The Lancet, 1988
Jama, 1950

between professional tattooists, due to the diverse views which they all hold with regard to the practice of their profession. For some, it is merely a business. For others, however, it is an art form inherited from the past, maintained with respect and passed on by masters. They feel that there is a big difference between standard designs which are reproduced over and over again like transfers, and the unique creative work, which is drawn free-hand, rather than copied.

In France a tattooing association was established in 1986 with the aim of regulating tattooing practice. This association has drawn up a list of professional tattooists in France, as well as a code of ethics for tattooists, the most important elements of which stipulate that:

* Every dermaplastician who is a member of the French Tattooing Association should observe the following rules:
   -Do not tattoo a minor or anyone who pre sents a health risk
   -Refuse to tattoo any motif which is not aesthetically pleasing or any motifs in a place on the body which might jeopardise the customer's integrity
   -Assume the role of consultant to the customer (with regard to choice of motifs, colours, positioning, etc.)

* Every dermaplastician who is a member of the French Tattooing Association guarantees that the basic rules of hygiene will be observed as follows:

   -The equipment is always cleaned and disinfected after each customer
   -Needle sets are cleaned and needle tips are changed after each customer
   -Ink containers are disposed of after each customer
   -Surgical gloves should always be worn
   -Work should always be carried out on anti-septic surfaces with a pedal activitated water basin and soap dispenser close at hand

* Smoking is not permitted in the tattooing area, and a sign should be posted to that effect

There are about 150 authorised tattooists practising their trade in France, but there are also about 3,000 unauthorised ones, not including the occasional amateurs or those in the prisons.

Therefore the best advice for those who wish to be tattooed is to visit a well-known, authorised, professional artist.

In France, where there is no formal tattooing training, tattooists usually gain all their experience by working an apprenticeship with more experienced artists, and often take the opportunity to perfect their techniques at international tattooing conventions. These conventions provide a meeting place for specialists from all over the world, whatever their level of skill. The artists discuss technique, needle size and colour combinations, and buy catalogues of motifs. People who are already covered in tattoos come to the conventions to seek out the famous masters of the craft to supplement their existing decorations. Those who have no experience whatsoever of tattooing, but are curious, come to investigate, and many leave with their first tattoo as a souvenir. The clothing worn at these events is usually that which is the most appropriate for the occasion - transparent fabrics, mini skirts, low-cut garments and dresses with holes cut in them to show off the tattoos beneath. The men usually walk around topless. The atmosphere is feverish, exotic............

The convention is a type of congress - a forum for the professionals - which attempts to dispel the negative stereotyping prevalent in tattooing, to dispense information on artistic tattooing practice and to promote its acceptance by the majority. There are tattooing museums in Tokyo, San Francisco and Amsterdam. The Amsterdam museum was opened by Hanky Panky, world traveller and generally colourful character, who also happens to be an excellent tattooist.

The master tattooists in Europe include Philippe Leu in Lausanne, Bernie Lüther and Klaus Führman in Vienna and Phil Bond in the UK. Bruno of Pigalle remains the most well known of the French tattooists, having always had a high profile in the media. However, at the first international tattooing convention in Paris in 1991, Tintin from Toulouse was awarded the honour of best tattooist in France. In the USA Ed Hardy, Cliff Raven and Léo Zulueta are the leaders in the field. The Horiyoshi family has reigned over the tattooing world in Japan for three generations since the turn of the century.

One of the less desirable side effects of tattooing is the allergic reaction which can be produced by the metallic salts used to produce the various colours. These reactions, although difficult to anticipate, are becoming more and more rare, thanks to the increasing use of hypoallergenic substances. The colour red (obtained from cinnabar) and green (obtained from chrome) can cause swelling and a rash to occur. Consequently, as the pigment is fixed in the skin for good, these symptoms result in a permanent irritation. There are creams available which can alleviate the itching temporarily, but the only real cure is to remove the tattoo.

Tattoo removal

The removal of a tattoo, regardless of the technique used, always leaves an ugly scar.

The process of tattoo removal is as old as the art of tattooing itself. Lists of corrosive substances which were used to remove the identification tattoos of Greek slaves are recorded in the works of Plato

The desire to remove tattoos usually corresponds with a change of circumstances. The tattooed individual needs to erase painful memories of the past and is seeking rehabilitation by means of a redemptive catharsis. His tattoo has either become psychologically embarrassing because of changes in his social position, or it has turned out to be physically uncomfortable because it has caused chronic irritation.

There are various methods of erasing these marks which, for one reason or another, have become burdensome. The most common methods include the application of caustic products, surgery followed by skin graft, rotating pumice wheel and freezing with liquid nitrogen - all of which are done under anaesthetic. The method used depends on the size, location and type of tattoo design.

The most up-to-date tattoo removal procedure using a CO_2 laser is the preferred method of most doctors and tattooed individuals. Nevertheless, the laser still causes a burn, the severity of which corresponds to the depth to which the tattoo has been injected. Tattoos undertaken by professional, experienced tattooists apparently remain closer to the surface of the skin.

None of these techniques is ideal in the physical sense, but their success sometimes lies in the more psychological view of the process in which the removal represents a sort of magic, purifying act, so that the scar is not a humiliating mark at all. On the contrary, it adds value to the individual's attempt at reintegration. It provides a lasting souvenir, so that the tattoo is never really negated.

The tattoo is a unique object - a naive and provocative moving fresco. Born out of pain, it bursts out of a tear in the skin, takes shape and expands to the rhythm of the punctures. It is a creative but cruel delight, an object of desire or fear. It allows us to enter into an unknown world, quite different to that evoked by the basic, clumsy tattoos of a stormy adolescence.

A flower blooms from the navel, a wave breaks against the breast, a spider weaves its web around the elbow, which folds and unfolds it, as if it

SKIN OF THE SOUL...

were supporting it against the wind or positioning it to trap its prey.

But the initial surprise which these strange colour prints might evoke does not detract from the one overwhelming fact that they are fixed, imperishable, indelible.

One can be hypnotised by the splendour of these mobile canvasses, fixing the skin with an unwavering gaze, or one can simply be carried away by emotions. Some people are shocked by the bewildering strangeness of these decorations and the monstrous metamorphosis which they represent. But one can also try to understand...Hasn't man always tried to unravel the mystery of destiny, in order to master it?

Symbolic expression may be a way of unveiling the mystery, of facing up to the future. Perhaps tattooing represents Ariadne's thread with which man can find his way through his labyrinth?

In order to plumb the mysterious depths of the human soul, maybe, like Alice, we should be tempted into Wonderland, even though we risk some unpleasant encounters along the route which is mapped out by this thread of images?

CREDITS

ACTORS
All the people photographed were present at the first French international tattooing convention.

French tattooists of the French Tattooing Association
Alain, Lorient
Jo Marina, Nantes
J-M Tattoo, Rennes
Bop John, Bourges
Gilles Tatouage, Brest
Tintin Universal Tattoo, Toulouse
Stéphane Fröhring, Balogne

Other tattooists
Marco Pisa, Bologne, Italy
Mauricio Fercionni, Milan, Italy
Johnny Nielsen, Amsterdam, Holland
Hanky Panky - Ronald Bonkerk, Amsterdam, Holland
Travelin Berni, Vienna, Austria
Philippe Tatouage, Grand Sacconex, Switzerland
Tattoo Bertje, Ostende, Belgium
Weber's Tattoo, Berlin, Germany
Sting's Tätowier Studio, Bremerhaven, Germany
Kevin Shercliff, Hednesford, UK
Derek Campbell, London, UK
Bugs Tattoo, London, UK
Brian Everett - Fine Line Tattoo, Albuquerque, USA
Jack Rudy, Anaheim, USA
Jonathan Shaw, New York, USA

MAKE-UP ARTIST: Véronique Maisière
HAIR: Lenny
TECHNICAL ADVISERS: Michel Petrovski
Dominique Grognard
SECURITY: Hell's Angels
DESIGNER: Dominique Isoird
PHOTOGRAPHY: Claudio Lazi
PHOTOGRAPHER'S ASSISTANT:
Olivier Rahard
DIRECTOR: Dr. Catherine Grognard

NOTES

NOTES

NOTES